The Fundamentals of Branding

Melissa Davis

ava
academia

An AVA Book

Published by AVA Publishing SA
Rue des Fontenailles 16
Case Postale
1000 Lausanne 6
Switzerland
Tel: +41 786 005 109
Email: enquiries@avabooks.ch

Distributed by Thames & Hudson (ex-North America)
181a High Holborn
London WC1V 7QX
United Kingdom
Tel: +44 20 7845 5000
Fax: +44 20 7845 5055
Email: sales@thameshudson.co.uk
www.thamesandhudson.com

Distributed in the USA & Canada by:
Ingram Publisher Services Inc.
1 Ingram Blvd.
La Vergne TN 37086
USA
Tel: +1 866 400 5351
Fax: +1 800 838 1149
Email: customer.service@ingrampublisherservices.com

English Language Support Office
AVA Publishing (UK) Ltd.
Tel: +44 1903 204 455
Email: enquiries@avabooks.ch

ISBN 978-2-940373-98-7

10 9 8 7 6 5 4 3 2 1

Design by Matthew Robertson / Other Rooms

Production by AVA Book Production Pte. Ltd., Singapore
Tel: +65 6334 8173
Fax: +65 6259 9830
Email: production@avabooks.com.sg

All reasonable attempts have been made to trace,
clear and credit the copyright holders of the images
reproduced in this book. However, if any credits have
been inadvertently omitted, the publisher will endeavour
to incorporate amendments in future editions.

Melissa Davis

The Fundamentals
of Branding

Ethical: aware-
ness/
reflect-
ion/
debate

academia

Contents

1

2

3

4

5

6

+

How to get the most
out of this book

The Fundamentals of Branding is intended
to give the reader an overview of branding
and brand structures in an easily digestible
way. It is based on insight from branding
professionals and from working within the
industry. This book can be used by both
students and people in business who seek
to gain practical knowledge and theoretical
insights about the discipline of branding.

Case studies and images of brands are
used throughout the book to demonstrate
different approaches to brands and
branding. Exercises are also included in
every chapter to help the reader reflect on
what they have learnt; these also offer an
opportunity to be creative.

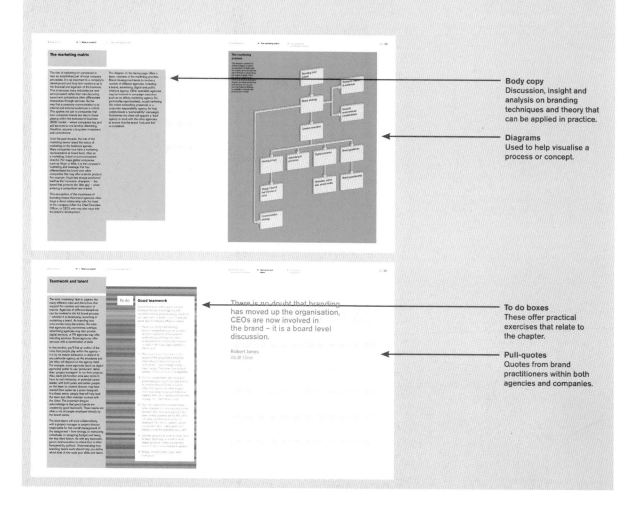

Body copy
Discussion, insight and
analysis on branding
techniques and theory that
can be applied in practice.

Diagrams
Used to help visualise a
process or concept.

To do boxes
These offer practical
exercises that relate to
the chapter.

Pull-quotes
Quotes from brand
practitioners within both
agencies and companies.

Box-outs
A more in-depth insight into a particular area of branding that is related to that chapter.

Images
Images come from a range of local and international brands to highlight points or concepts in the text.

Case studies
Offer extra analysis on a particular brand to demonstrate an evolving area of branding.

Interviews
Highlight the views of leading experts across different areas of branding.

What is a brand?

1

Defining branding

The terms brand and branding are now commonly used in everyday vocabulary; yet, they are also terms that are often misinterpreted. In recent years, branding has become a fundamental part of companies, organisations and even individuals. It is now so closely linked to the workings of a company, that if a brand suffers damage, so too does the company. On the other hand, a strong brand will boost the value of the company.

But what exactly is a brand? It is much more than a logo or a name. A brand represents the full 'personality' of the company and is the interface between a company and its audience. A brand may come into contact with its audience in various ways: from what we see and hear, through to our physical experiences with the brand and general feelings or perceptions we have about a company. A brand encapsulates both the tangible and the intangible and can be applied to almost anything – a person (like David Beckham), a business (Apple, Coca-Cola, Microsoft), a country, or even a nebulous idea (George Bush's 'War on Terror' or Britain's short-lived 'Cool Britannia' in the 1990s). The products, services and people of an organisation or entity are all part of the brand and affect the way that audiences both perceive and interact with a given brand.

Brand and business

The term 'branding' is often used as a catch-all to define many things, from the general marketing of a product to a name change or logo creation. Developing a brand that is sustainable requires a deep understanding of how that business, organisation or person operates. The branding process offers a backbone to the business by helping to define the company's position in its market (including its place among its competitors), and a direction and vision for the business. Once this is established, a brand strategy can be formulated which acts as a blueprint for the business and further defines areas such as audiences and brand values. In essence, a brand is the encapsulation of a company's core value as well as representing its aspirations and aims. It must be an accurate and authentic reflection of the business and should be visible to employees as well as to customers.

Brand and society

Flexibility and adaptability are key attributes for any brand that wants to survive in a constantly changing society and global marketplace. This does not mean that a company must rebrand within a new economic climate or when entering a new national market. However, a company will often adjust the way it positions itself to new audiences, particularly if entering new markets. For example, Korean electronics company, Samsung, was initially perceived in Europe throughout the 1990s as a lower-end brand because its products were cheaper. In Moscow, meanwhile, it was viewed as an elite brand. Samsung now rivals Sony as a high-quality, consumer electronics brand.

Brand and change

A brand must also respond to shifts in social trends to remain in tune with its audience. Significant shifts so far this century include the rapid development of new forms of technology, including social media networks (such as MySpace and Facebook), and responding to global issues such as climate change.

Upheavals in society, as well as new technologies, have significantly altered the relationship between brands and their audiences over the past decade. There has been a breaking down of barriers where many brands have shifted from speaking directly to audiences to engaging with them.

Audiences now seek a dialogue with brands instead – and this can take the form of influencing the brand through pressure, voicing opinions about the brand's products or services, or co-creating a product or service. Many people now expect a deeper connection with brands and greater transparency about the business that sits behind the brand. Yet even in our rapidly changing world, the fundamental principles of branding and brand management still apply.

The clothing brand, Gap, started in California in 1969 and now has over 3,000 stores worldwide. Its casual lifestyle brand image (as seen in the ad, above) has been central to its success. Like many retailers, the company has had its ups and downs, including reports of poor labour practices.

Case study
Google

Technology brands now have a dominant presence within the world's top brands. Brands such as Google, Facebook and MySpace have appeared within the past decade to become internationally used and recognised brands.

The international growth and strength of Google's brand in its short ten-year lifespan is phenomenal. Google was not the first search engine in cyberspace (brands such as AltaVista and Yahoo! were popular search engines at the time that Google entered the market), but its superior search capability made it hugely popular. The brand is constantly extending into other areas of technology such as 'cloud computing', location-based functions and applications such as Google Earth and its web browser, Chrome. Its online existence also gives the brand greater flexibility – such as being able to update its logo as the seasons change. Google's website boasts that it has become 'one of the world's best known brands almost entirely through word of mouth'.

The brand status accorded to technology brands such as Google may still seem a little surprising in the traditional branding world. Yet Google offers all the emotional and functional attributes of any 'real world' brand – a cool status, quality and adaptability. It also promotes a strong culture of brand identity and affiliation within the company.

Google's logos (above) are as versatile as its brand. Its main logo sometimes changes with the seasons. The company also constantly introduces new technology services that are instantly recognisable.

Case study
McDonald's

The way we consume food today is very different from when McDonald's first emerged in 1955. People are now more health-aware; there is pressure on food companies to reduce rising levels of obesity, yet McDonald's still remains one of the world's largest brands.

The brand has undergone a relatively significant transformation in the 21st century and is also accorded a different status across different countries as new markets emerge. In Europe, for example, McDonald's has tried to address its fast food, unhealthy image by changing its menu and the style of its restaurants to be more café-like and its branding to be more subtle. Meanwhile, in India, McDonald's has the elite status of a Western brand that is frequented by the Indian middle classes.

Whether you're 'lovin' it' or not (as the strapline goes), McDonald's still has a huge influence as a brand and is currently ranked as the eighth most popular brand in the world, according to Interbrand's Best Global Brands poll of 2008.

McDonald's is a brand that is internationally recognized but accorded a different status around the world by its customers. In Taiwan (top) and Shanghai (bottom), it is viewed as an elite brand, appealing more to the local middle classes and tourists.

i'm lovin' it™

Brand history

Brands have been around for a long time. They were used centuries ago as an identifier for ownership – from branding horses to slaves. The emergence of brands in the commercial world most probably started at the end of the 19th century after the Industrial Revolution.

Many of today's well-known brands – such as Ford, P&G (Procter & Gamble) and Dutch home electronics brand, Philips – started life as family-owned businesses. Philips, for example, began in Holland in 1891 as a lighting business before going on to become a multinational manufacturer of electronics and medical equipment.

There was also a wave of social pioneers in the 19th century that introduced social values into business and set up brands such as Cadbury's, Rowntree, financial company Friends Provident and the bank that is now LloydsTSB. It seems that few brands today remain family-owned although a brand's heritage is still a core part of its story. Many brands play on the fact that they remain committed to their roots and the values (social or otherwise) of their founders. This sense of brand lineage can provide a strong story for a brand.

An early TV set from Philips (top), one of the pioneers of home technology. More recent innovations include the Pocket Travel Light (above) and the Digi Cam keyring (right). Philips prides itself on bringing good quality, well-designed products to a mass audience.

Cadbury's (right) started in 1824 in Birmingham, UK. From humble beginnings as a high-street store it is now one of the largest confectionery businesses in the world. The brand is no longer family-owned but the company still promotes the social principles of its Quaker founder, John Cadbury.

The early days of branding

The concept of brand management and marketing systems, like that of research and development, emerged around the 1920s and 1930s with competing companies such as General Motors and Ford creating cars for a growing mass market. Consumer goods company, P&G, was a leader in researching audience preferences for its growing consumer brands.

However, it was undoubtedly the growth of post-war economies and an expanding middle class that gave impetus to brands and a rising consumerism. This was followed by a boom in advertising in the 1980s, driven by agencies like Saatchi & Saatchi. During the 1990s, with further media proliferation and increasing competition among products and services, branding (in Western markets) became an essential part of business for both consumer-facing and business brands. Branding helps businesses stand out and offers audiences some understanding of the product or service on offer.

Brand growth in new markets, such as China and India, is evident as people's living standards increase and a thriving middle class flocks to global brands. Economic prosperity within these markets also offers new scope for luxury brands – which are currently facing a downturn in troubled Western markets.

Today's brand landscape

The last two decades have been critical to the brand environment that we see now. Many of today's larger global brands have been formed through a more recent history of mergers and acquisitions, particularly since the 1990s. The dot-com wave of the late 1990s also gave birth to new online brands – those with little substance behind them failed to survive when the dot-com bubble burst. Common government tactics, such as the deregulation of industries like postal services, telecoms and railways, have also opened up particular sectors for competition and the emergence of new brands. The more recent burgeoning of private equity funds and venture capital has enabled smaller successful brands to grow quickly through cash injections. And, of course, the growth of the media over the past two decades has also influenced brand ubiquity.

Branding diversity

What has also changed in today's brand landscape is that dominant brands are no longer limited to corporations – brands from the charity sector, such as Oxfam, Amnesty and Greenpeace now have huge global presences. Celebrity culture has also driven the rise of 'personality brands' like the Beckhams', those of various supermodels and even of politicians, such as Barack Obama – in these cases, the person's public-facing identity is carefully crafted through looks, values and associations.

New 'brandscapes'

During the late 1980s and 1990s, Japanese and Korean brands started transforming the international 'brandscape', with brands such as Sony and Samsung entering Europe and the US. In the past decade, brands from China and India have started to make an international impact and also serve huge home markets. Huawei, for example, is a key player in the telecoms sector. It began in China in 1988 and entered the European market in 2000 offering full telecom services. *BusinessWeek* has acknowledged it as one of the world's most influential companies.

Branding in 2020

It is highly likely that by 2020 the landscape of brands will have changed again, as further shifts in both economic power and societal trends occur. The US and Europe's financial crisis has coincided with a desire to consume less, alongside pressing environmental issues such as climate change. This is forcing brands to adapt their messages and innovate their products (for example, by introducing 'green' products). The crisis may also result in some new economic models for business; and runs parallel with the rapid growth of new consumer markets in Eastern and central Europe, China, India and Latin America. The eventual future outlook may result in a more international diversity of leading brands on the world stage, rather than the global dominance of US and European-owned brands currently seen.

Chinese company Huawei
is a key player in the
telecoms sector and a
global leader in mobile
network equipment, with
14 research & development
centres around the world.
Recent Huawei advertising
campaigns (above).

Haier is another leading
Chinese technology brand
and ranks within the top five
of the world's white goods
manufacturers. Pictured is
Haier's central building in
Qingdao, China (right).

Haier

How branding has changed

As brands and branding as a discipline has matured, so too has the relationship with brand audiences. Brand approaches constantly evolve to engage audiences at different levels. Branding has shifted from being simply about 'identity creation' – that is, designing a logo, name and 'look and feel' for the brand – to a period of attempting to emotionally connect with audiences (for example, McDonald's 'I'm lovin' it' strapline; Nike's 'Just Do It' and Apple's 'Think Different'). But today's audience still expects more.

The brand experience

Audience sophistication led to the concept of the 'brand experience', which brings together both the tangible and intangible elements of the brand through various 'touchpoints'. A brand experience endeavours to engage people with the brand at a level that captures the audience's senses. This idea also helps competing brands stand out from one another – airlines, for example, may offer similar prices on a route but promise different flying experiences.

The brand experience still matters, particularly where service is a differentiator. But branding now is moving into a phase where brands need to demonstrate their ability to deliver in addition to emphasising their values. Areas such as a brand response to environmental and social causes, or great design, can help differentiate a brand. In a leaner economic climate, the functional attributes of a brand, such as its quality, service and ability to deliver on its 'brand promise' will also stand out.

Brand progression

As brands emerge and develop – and many do not survive – it is critical that they stay ahead of their audience and reflect the society in which they exist. Brands often reinvent themselves to do this. However, a reinvention does not necessarily require a full 'rebrand' or changing of a logo and name but can, instead, be done by 'repositioning' the brand. For example, Nike's 'Just Do It' strapline was an addition to the brand mark and became synonymous with the Nike brand and its focus on athletes, rather than product.

Other brands, such as the charity, Action for Children, opted for a new name and image in 2008 when its old name eventually failed to create standout from other children's charities. The old name, National Children's Homes (NCH), also related to its origins as a children's orphanage, which was no longer relevant to the brand as it exists today.

Nike's 'Just Do It' strapline (right) has become iconic since it was launched in 1988 and has sustained 20 years of use. It was created by Wieden & Kennedy, Nike's long-standing advertising agency, at a time when Nike was losing market share to other footwear companies such as Reebok. The 'Just Do It' success lies in its simple bluntness and a huge amount of advertising dollars spent on promoting Nike 'heroes' rather than products.

Action for Children was set up in 1869 as an orphanage for homeless children on London's streets. Its modern-day role is to support and speak for children through community-based projects. Its logo has consistently been updated over the past century (left).

1906   **1964**   **1974**   **1994**   **2000**   **2008**

Case study
Mini brand heritage

The Mini was introduced in Britain in 1959 and became an icon of the 1960s. In 2001, the original Mini was transformed and reintroduced globally by BMW, owner of the rights to the Mini brand since buying Rover in 1994. Almost immediately, the Mini once again became an iconic car, featuring in various films and becoming popular among celebrities.

The transformation of the Mini shows that it is possible to make a 'heritage' brand contemporary, while retaining the original values and form of the brand. Importantly for BMW, the Mini never lost the cool status that it possessed in the 1960s, even when it was no longer in production. BMW successfully took a particularly British brand and redesigned everything, from the product itself to the brand 'look and feel', managing to retain the car's original values and status and yet propel it into a modern context.

The Mini was successfully relaunched in 2001 (top) while remaining true to the original car of the '60s (above). The revamped models also made an impact in the US market – while being perceived as quintessentially British. Its new convertible was introduced in March 2009 during a difficult period for the automotives sector.

Case study
Coca-Cola

Brands now exist in a multi-dimensional world where audiences have a range of choices and where business practices are more transparent. This can pose a challenge for many of the larger, high-profile brands.

Coca-Cola still ranks as one of the leading global brands but is having to adapt to a changing world where the brand may be unfamiliar to younger audiences; where greater awareness of health issues may make Coca-Cola less appealing to some audiences and where controversial business practice has been exposed by NGOs (non-governmental organisations).

Coca-Cola has recently announced a goal to become 'water neutral' in its business operations, after forming a partnership (in 2008) with the World Wildlife Fund. This announcement followed a court case in India where Coca-Cola was accused of taking water resources from local villages. Coca-Cola won the case, but the negative exposure still impacted on its reputation. The 'water neutral' announcement shows how companies are now taking steps to contribute proactively to society, in order to both protect their reputation and be seen as a leader in their market.

Coca-Cola often produces limited edition bottles or cans as collectors' items (above). Its original bottle design is iconic and the brand is frequently ranked as the world's most successful.

The marketing matrix

The role of marketing for companies is now an established part of most company processes. It is as important to a company's development and long-term existence as is the financial and legal arm of the business. This is because many industries are now service-based rather than manufacturing-based and competitors often differentiate themselves through services. So the way that a company communicates to its internal and external audiences is critical. This applies not just to companies that own consumer brands but also to those playing within the business-to-business (B2B) market – where companies buy and sell services to one another. Marketing, therefore, requires a long-term investment and commitment.

Over the past decade, the role of the marketing teams raised the status of marketing on the business agenda. Many companies now have a marketing representative at board level, often as a marketing, brand or communications director. For major global companies such as Virgin or Nike, it is the company's marketing and message that has differentiated the brand over other companies that may offer a similar product. For example, Virgin has always positioned itself as the 'consumer champion' – the brand that protects the 'little guy' – when entering a competitive new market.

This recognition of the importance of branding means that brand agencies often forge a direct relationship with the head of the company (often the Chief Executive Officer, or CEO) who may also input into the brand's development.

The diagram on the facing page offers a basic overview of the marketing process. Brand development tends to involve a number of different agencies, including a brand, advertising, digital and public relations agency. Other specialist agencies may be involved in campaign execution such as an affinity marketing agency (for partnership opportunities), social marketing (for online networking presence) or a corporate responsibility agency (to help communicate a 'sustainability' campaign). Sometimes the client will appoint a 'lead' agency to work with the other agencies to ensure that the brand 'look and feel' is consistent.

The marketing process

This diagram outlines the different stages of brand development. It starts with the briefing process with the client through to developing the brand strategy. There are various roles that fit within the creative execution stages, including advertising and naming. An ongoing communications strategy is needed to maintain the brand in the market.

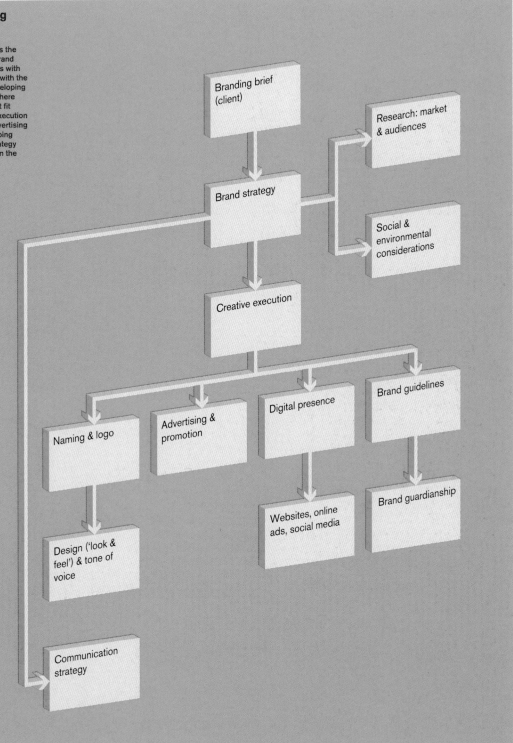

The basic brand development process

Large brands have complex management systems but tend to be tightly managed, with small close teams from the company and selected agencies working together. Any brand development is an investment for companies and will involve a step-by-step process. The level of depth of the process is also dependent on the project and the allocated budget.

Understanding the market in which the brand will operate, as well as the audience, is obviously critical for any brand. Market research and analysis is often applied at the outset of any brand project, and can be carried out through focus groups (offline or online) and market testing. The objective of most research is to support strategic decisions and provide a thorough understanding of the market.

Research offers raw information that should lead to insights about audience tastes and reactions to products, services, names and logos, for example, depending on the brief from the client. The results should feed into brand planning, the brand proposition and also into the creative development of the brand. Any final creative output should be checked against the original research to ensure that the brand is delivering to the audience.

The following stages outline the different skills involved when developing brands. This applies to creating new brands as well as to refreshing or updating brands.

Formulating a brand strategy

A brand strategy is critical to determine the direction for the brand. This may be managed 'in-house' (within the company itself) or done in tandem with an agency or brand consultants. As a general guide, it is often the branding agency, or lead marketing agency, that helps to create a brand strategy. A strategy should detail areas such as understanding the brand's audience, its market (including competitors) and should also integrate with the vision of the company. A company may also commission research into audience needs and experiences of the brand.

Creative execution: naming and logo

The strategy will feed into the brand development stage, which involves creating a look and feel for the brand, including the brand language (often referred to as its 'tone of voice') as well as the logo and name. An entire rebrand such as a name or logo change may not be necessary, but changing the visual aspects of the brand can reinvigorate or modernise it. This stage of the branding process tends to be carried out by the branding agency, which will have designers and writers as part of the team.

Creative implementation: advertising and digital presence

Brand implementation will involve advertising and design agencies. Advertising agencies still play a very powerful role in brand execution, often working in long-term collaborations with companies. In many cases, the ad agency will 'own' the brand's execution – the part that is visible on billboards, TV and in print. Design agencies are often key to the brand implementation process – and there are many smaller design agencies that will do full brand implementation, from concept to development. Some specialise in executing the brand online, which can involve a full translation of the brand to the digital sphere, with strategy and a creative process to ascertain how a brand should look, feel and communicate online. The digital presence of a brand is now as important as traditional advertising in the brand execution process.

Communicating the brand

A critical part of brand execution is defining how to best communicate the brand. Branding agencies should play a key role here, by developing a communications plan for the brand's ongoing presence. Some public relations agencies also specialise in this area. A communications strategy should cover both the employee and external communications execution for the brand.

German car manufacturer, Audi, has successfully differentiated itself as a high-end brand by emphasising design and technology – helped by its *Vorsprung durch Technik* strapline (roughly meaning 'leading by technique'). Like many leading car brands, it supports rally sports (top) – a great way for autobrands to demonstrate their technical expertise. A modern Audi convertible (above).

Teamwork and talent

The term 'marketing' fails to capture the many different roles and disciplines that support the creation and execution of brands. Agencies of different disciplines can be involved in the full brand process – whether it is developing, launching or sustaining a brand. As branding now runs across many disciplines, the roles that agencies play sometimes overlaps; advertising agencies may also provide digital services, or PR agencies may offer branding services. Some agencies offer services with a combination of skills.

In this section, you'll find an outline of the roles that people play within the agency – it is by no means exhaustive or distinct to any particular agency, as the structures and job titles will depend on the agency itself. For example, some agencies (such as digital agencies) prefer to use 'producers' rather than 'project managers' to run their projects. Also, each job function area also tends to have its own hierarchy, or potential career ladder, with both junior and senior people on the team (a creative director may have started their career as a junior designer). It is these senior people that will help lead the team and often maintain contact with the client. The important thing to acknowledge is that good brands are created by good teamwork. These teams are often a mix of people employed directly by the brand owner.

The best teams will work collaboratively, with a project manager or project director responsible for the overall management of the assignment – from timings, to instructing individuals, to assigning budget and being the key client liaison. As with any teamwork, good communication is critical (but is often hampered by politics). Understanding how branding teams work should help you define which kind of role suits your skills and talent.

To do

Good teamwork

Good teamwork within agencies and between the client and agency will inevitably lead to great branding results. It can also make or break a pitch. Here are some tips for creating effective teams:

→ Have a working methodology: brand management can be complex and time-sensitive. A transparent methodology will help the client understand the full process involved, as well as the team participating in the project.

→ Plan your project: be clear on the scope of the project and what the client should expect in terms of end results – even though things may change. This keeps the budget process transparent and manageable.

→ Use the whole team: developing or progressing a brand is not just limited to creative teams. Draw on talent within the agency for extra insight and ideas, such as people who have worked with other clients or those who manage the client relationship.

→ Use effective communication tools: what channels of communication exist between the client and agency? Are there online systems where the client can view updated work and post feedback? Are there systems which can involve other client teams and employees in the branding process?

→ Use the phone and communicate face-to-face: don't rely on email or web-based systems. Often a great idea needs to be communicated in person.

→ Always strive to make your client look good!

The basic brand
development process

▼ Teamwork and
talent

▶ The agency
playing field

28–29

There is no doubt that branding
has moved up the organisation,
CEOs are now involved in
the brand – it is a board level
discussion.

Robert Jones
Wolff Olins

The agency playing field

People working within agencies will offer a variety of skills and backgrounds. Generally, teams will include a mix of those in client management and brand strategy, as well as designers and writers. Cross-discipline teams offer a great resource for brand creativity.

At the outset, it is better to involve everyone who is working on the project in an ideas generation session (or brainstorm) to answer the brand brief. This means that the response to the brief will benefit from having people who understand the client well (such as the project managers), who can provide creative insight from other account work, or can offer a perspective from a different channel, such as the web.

The client manager/new business manager

This is the person responsible for attracting new clients, including getting on 'pitch lists'. Generally, they will be someone who has extensive agency experience, with a background in account management, sales or marketing. The client manager will often be the initial 'face' of the agency to the external world.

The project manager

The project manager – or senior project manager – will hold the account together. They are the key person who will talk to the client and make sure that the project is delivered on time and to a specific brief. Of course, in the real world, projects often overrun and budgets can be over-exhausted. It is the project manager's role to assess timings and keep control of the budget.

The strategists

Some branding and design agencies have a strategy team, often the 'thinkers' behind the projects, responsible for ensuring that the brand direction is in line with the company vision. Strategy plays a critical role and heavily influences the creative output of the brand. It determines the positioning and direction of the brand – such as how it will be different from competitors. The strategy team should work closely with the creative team.

The digital specialists

Digital teams – those that create the brand online – will interpret the traditional brand to the online environment for websites, banners, online advertisements and other forms of digital media. In some cases, the online development of the brand will drive the direction of the brand, as the digital space becomes more prominent, and thus more critical to many brands.

The 'creatives'

The creative team are often referred to as those who literally create the brand through words and images. In general terms, a creative team will include the designers and copywriters, but may also include specialist skills such as those of product or digital designers. They make the brand come to life by working with the strategy and project management team.

The production teams

The production specialists are those that ensure that the brand is delivered in various formats to enable its presence in print, TV, digital spaces and other forms of media. These people are the production specialists or programmers. They work closely with the creative teams and project management to ensure that the brand is executed in the best way possible.

Case study
Interbrand

Interbrand is an international branding agency best known for its brand strategy and evaluation abilities. The company pioneered measuring techniques for branding in the 1980s during the era of some high-profile mergers and acquisitions (M&As) of brands that were formerly not recognised for their values.

It has also been an important leader in progressing the idea of branding from straight 'identity' work, such as logo and naming development, to making the value of brands a key part of business and an important business asset.

Each year, Interbrand releases its top 100 brand ranking list. Companies are measured according to the brand's international presence, financial data and potential future earnings. Interbrand then quantifies a net value for the brand. Applying this kind of hard and factual criteria to brands has strengthened the role of brands within business.

Interbrand is one of the leading branding agencies and is globally recognised. It is well known for its brand evaluation strength.

It recently updated Barclays Bank's retail brand, working on the positioning, visual identity, brand architecture and tone of voice (top). It also refreshed the visual identity for Toyota in 2004 (left).

Interbrand

◀ Teamwork and
talent

▼ **The agency
playing field**

▷ The client/agency
relationship

32–33

Case study
Saatchi & Saatchi

While advertising agencies differ from
branding agencies, they have played an
enormous role in the rise of brands since the
1980s – the boom days of the advertising
sector. Perhaps the most well-known agency
during this time was Saatchi & Saatchi.

Set up by two brothers, Maurice and
Charles, the agency made its name with
bold campaigns in the early 1980s. The
agency's fame was built on its advertising
for the UK's Conservative Party in the
election that brought Margaret Thatcher to
power. Saatchi & Saatchi dominated the
advertising world for around two decades,
until the brothers left in the mid 1990s. It is
still a leading global agency.

Advertising agencies play a fundamental
role in brand expression and also influence
particular trends in brand language. For
years, agencies have also touted the idea
of 'cross-platform' campaigns – campaigns
that work across the digital space and
offline. Online media offers a strong growth
area for traditional advertising agencies.

Saatchi & Saatchi was
credited with winning the
election campaign for the
UK's Conservative Party
in 1979, with this 'poster
ad of the century', as
voted for by UK industry
magazine *Campaign*.
Saatchi & Saatchi's T-Mobile
campaign of 2009 used
the brand's strapline 'Life's
for sharing', 'flash mobs'
and social media to create
'spontaneous' performances.
The ad (top) was filmed in
a London tube station
in 2009.

SAATCHI & SAATCHI

The client/agency relationship

Brand development is often outsourced from a company to an agency. Therefore, the relationship between the client and the agency that delivers the project is critical. Any agency must start by understanding the workings, values and direction of the business behind the brand. This will help create the 'essence' of a brand and also define its aspirations. This, in turn, makes its positioning clear to the audience: contemporary (Tiffanys), environmentally conscious (BP) or accessible to all (Zara, Mango, Uniqlo).

Innovation is also key in branding, no matter what the economic climate. Agencies can play a key role in creating something different by being involved at the initial conceptual stage, as the Mr & Mrs Smith boutique leisure brand demonstrates.

Mr & Mrs Smith is a guidebook concept created for discerning couples who want an insight into great places to stay, including boutique hotels. It is based on the idea of a couple checking in under the widely-used pseudonym, 'Mr & Mrs Smith' and leave anonymous reviews. The brand was created by Bloom Design, who developed the positioning, name and identity of the concept. Its launch in 2003 offered a new approach to the travel review sector. It has since become an international brand delivered online and across various media, as well as offering a guest booking service.

The key to a good relationship

A long-term, happy relationship between client and agency is dependent upon transparency and excellent client communication. In many cases, a client will manage the brand while working with an agency that will be responsible for the ongoing development and application of that brand. This means that a company (the brand owner) will invest more than time and money in the client/agency relationship – much of the value is often through personal relationships between the client and agency as well.

The temptation for many companies is to outsource the creative direction of the brand while the brand owner will hold the reins on the brand identity and its direction. An organisation may work with a number of agencies at once. A good agency will have a clear vision for the brand that comes from the company itself, and fits in with the company vision. Brands such as Nike and Apple have strong ownership of their brand identity and its direction.

The business of pitching

The majority of marketing-based agencies (branding, design and public relations) will undertake a 'pitch' process to win a client. This can be a costly and time-consuming – but necessary – exercise for agencies, particularly when pitching for work from large corporate or public sector brands. Some organisations, particularly in the public sector, are obliged to put work out for tender at regular intervals.

◀ The agency
playing field

▼ The client/agency
relationship

▷ Brand structures

34–35

Mr & Mrs Smith is a concept
created for couples who want
to stay in boutique hotels,
based on the idea of a couple
who check in under the
widely used pseudonym. It
has become an international
brand delivered online and
across various media (right
and below).

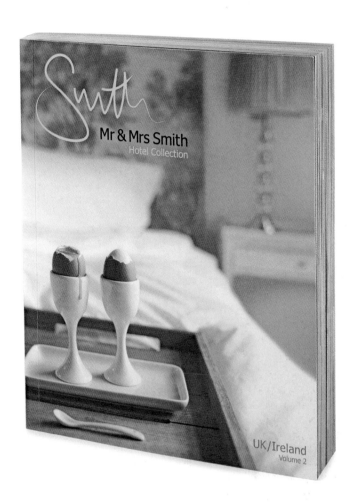

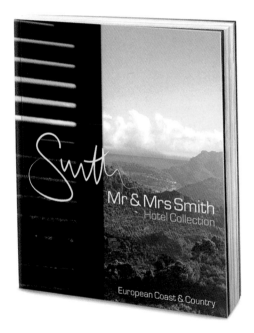

The pitch process

There are no hard and fast rules for pitching but, generally, an agency will first provide credentials to determine whether they are able to fulfil the client brief based on the individual personalities involved in the pitch. If they are invited to pitch, agencies often provide brand and design concepts as well as details on their methodology. This gives the client an insight into how the agency will work and how strong their ideas are. Personalities and presentation skills are also a factor – sometimes a client will determine the winning agency based on the team involved in the pitch.

Potential pitfalls

The closeness of the relationship between client and agency means that it is important that ground rules are established from the outset. A common client frustration is that the team who pitches for a brand project changes once the job is appointed; that senior people are replaced with those who are less experienced; or that the scope of work is underestimated and therefore costs more.

To avoid this, those responsible for taking the brief from the client should aim to maintain some consistency in the people who offer the skills and talent for the client. It is also the role of the agency to ensure that the energy and promises delivered during the pitch are maintained right through to the final delivery of the project. This may be difficult in reality, but a good client/ agency relationship can be long-lasting.

Bringing the brand to life

A mistake often made is that a brand project is deemed to be complete once the name, logo and brand execution are delivered. Yet, the ongoing communications and maintenance of the brand are as critical as the brand development stage. A failure to execute the brand correctly both within and outside of the company can seriously damage a brand. This is often down to poor or confusing communications.

Branding agencies have an opportunity to take responsibility for communicating the brand to employees as well as to other stakeholders. They can also play a role in helping to maintain the application of the brand, by acting as 'brand guardians'; that is, ensuring that the brand is applied correctly through other mediums, from its digital application through to product design.

Inter-agency relationships

Generally, a large company will work with a number of specialised agencies or consultants to help execute certain aspects of the brand. This can include digital and social media agencies, through to brand or corporate responsibility advisors. The range of talent involved across brand executions is indicative of how prominent branding has now become and of its increasing overlap into a number of different arenas. When times are tough economically, budgets may be tight – but projects are still outsourced, nevertheless. The key for agencies or freelancers is to offer value and stability while continuing to innovate and push the brand forward.

◀ The agency
playing field

▼ The client/agency
relationship

▷ Brand structures

36–37

Case study
02 & Lambie-Nairn

The mobile phone brand, O2, was formed
in 2001 after a demerger from BT's former
mobile business. Branding agency Lambie-
Nairn helped create the new brand and
has since been responsible for the 'brand
guardianship' of O2, which includes working
with O2 to manage the ongoing direction
and design of the O2 brand execution
across its various markets.

This kind of guardianship role is becoming
more common between agencies and
companies (the brand owners). It puts the
branding agency in a strong position as
the client relationship tends to be long-
term. However appointing an agency as
brand guardians will only work if both the
client and lead agency are respected when
working with the other agencies.

As O2's lead branding agency, we
oversee all the creative work developed
for the brand across all of its markets,
working on numerous different projects
at once. Agencies send us a working
brief with initial concepts and we feed
back on the creative work until it's in
production. We also release the relevant
brand 'assets' as and when agencies
need them.

However, there is a fine line for us to
tread: we have to be careful about giving
creative direction to agencies, when all
the agencies are creative. Our role is to
retain the integrity of the brand whilst
allowing it to evolve in the right direction.

Nicky Nicolls
Client services director / Lambie-Nairn

O2 has recently updated
its brand identity through
new styles of advertising
and products and has
benefited from its exclusive
relationship with Apple's
iPhone. O2's new ad style
(top) and the iPhone
(right).

Deconstructing brands

Brand structures

Brand structure is also known as brand architecture and provides a map of relationships between all of the brands in a company's portfolio. It helps companies to define the relationship between the different brands and provides an overview that is easily managed. The brand structure will cover a picture of the whole brand 'family', including the relationship between the parent brand and its sub-brands, the relationships among sub-brands themselves and also to brand extensions.

A brand structure helps the brand manager understand the role and contribution of each brand to the overall success of the business. It can facilitate decisions on how to invest in specific brands, or whether they should be disposed of, rebranded or retired. It should also offer a clear view of which brands are owned by whom, as well as the distinctive benefits of each brand.

Types of brand structures

Brand structures are not necessarily visible to the customer and may not impact on their choice of brand. For example, large consumer-goods companies such as P&G or Unilever both own a number of different fast-moving consumer goods (FMCG) brands (including toiletries and home care products like washing powder). Brands within the same family may also compete with each other for the consumer's wallet.

Coherence

A coherent brand structure can positively benefit individual brands, by making it clear what the brands stand for. This means that the consumer can transfer their trust in one brand onto others within the group. For example, the success of the Apple iPod resulted in many Apple converts to its desktop Macs and laptops – people who would never previously have tried the Apple operating system. Other brands, such as the Virgin Group, stand for particular values that are in favour of supporting the consumer, values which are then applied to every sub-brand within the group.

While the tendency for brand managers (particularly of Western brands) is to extend products in an identifiable, coherent way – where a clothing brand may move into home interiors, for example – this systematic approach matters less outside of Western environments. The Tata Group in India, for example, best known for its trucks and heavy vehicles, also makes jewellery, bottled water and owns hotel chains. The product mix has little in common apart from the Tata name. Kingfisher, an Indian brewery brand, owns an airline. Within India, these brands are respected as large brand names, with strong personalities and quality products.

The Virgin brand family (below) is recognised internationally and comprises over 200 companies. Richard Branson, its founder, is a master entrepreneur and has built much of the success of his brand around his informal personality and the brand's stance of being the 'consumer champion'. The demise of some Virgin brands (such as Virgin Brides) has not detracted from the overall brand image or success.

Tata is another global brand
spearheaded by a strong
personality. Still a family-
owned business, it came to
international attention when
it bought the very British
Jaguar brand (now the
Jaguar Land Rover group)
and Corus, formerly British
Steel (and now a subsidiary
of Tata Steel).

Tata's ever-growing
presence extends from
making cars (facing page)
and trucks (top left) to
Himalayan water (above),
hotel rooms (top right)
and tea. Its numerous
sub-brands bear little
resemblance to each other,
but are still known as part
of the Tata Group.

The Tata Nano car (above
right) was launched in March
2009 as a smaller, cheaper
and lighter car expected to
have a large following.

The parent brand

Some brands now invest in making the 'parent' brand visible to the consumer, where previously the corporate brand was only relevant to the investor community and employees. Drinks brand owner, Diageo, for example, has become a well-known brand, even though its product brands are more relevant to the consumer.

The parent brand can carry distinct associations and attributes – such as promoting a key message or identity. In Diageo's case, the brand has been used to carry a message to consumers of 'responsible drinking'. This message has also been carried throughout the sub-brands. The parent brand may also be identified with an overall 'promise' and values to customers, to provide a consistent experience and performance that runs through the brands. This forms the basis of a trusted relationship with the stakeholders.

Types of portfolios

Brand structures differ a lot among the global brands. Older, larger brands such as the consumer goods companies, Unilever and P&G, have a complex relationship among the brands within the company. This may present a confused picture to their audiences but generally people will buy into a particular product.

Decisions will be made among the portfolio as to whether to 'sell off' excess or non-aligned brands, integrate them, rebrand them or keep them as they are. In some cases, brands may be bought to boost an overall portfolio – such as adding an 'ethical' brand to a mainstream portfolio. In this case, the acquired brand may have an incredibly strong identity in its own right and its core brand values and attributes left untouched.

Acquiring brands

Brands are often added to and dumped from portfolios to extend a product range or make it more targeted. However, acquiring brands can potentially backfire when a large multinational corporation purchases a smaller, niche brand. If it is going to work, the audience must view the association as credible, or the niche brand must be allowed to retain its identity.

L'Oréal acquired The Body Shop in 2006, when The Body Shop's brand reputation as an environmentally conscious, pro-Fairtrade company (set up and formerly owned by the entrepreneur and social activist Dame Anita Roddick) was firmly established. However, there was concern amongst some Body Shop customers that its strong ethical stance against animal testing, its vocal promotion of human rights and support for local communities would not continue to be adopted by L'Oréal, the world's largest cosmetics brand and one that formerly had animal-testing policies.

Pret A Manger – a UK sandwich chain – was partly (and temporarily) acquired by McDonald's in 2001. This led to some negative associations with the Pret brand, even though there was no tangible evidence of McDonald's presence within the shops.

In reality, many corporations acquire smaller, niche brands to both invest in them and expand their presence, but no longer dabble with the core values and brand ingredients of the smaller brand. This way, they can retain an existing, core audience and also bring in new customers by injecting some energy into the brand and making it more visible.

The Body Shop is still one
of the world's leading brands
despite tough competition
in the natural cosmetics
market (above and right). Its
acquisition by L'Oréal may
have damaged its reputation
but the value of shares in the
company soared.

Prior to the acquisition,
the brand was becoming
dated and needed to attract
a new audience. L'Oréal
maintained that it would
invest in growing the brand
and has left the brand's
values untouched.

Brand families

Brand hierarchy structures can be used to group brands into families. This helps brand owners to identify market opportunities and extend the brand, if necessary, using a number of techniques.

Here are some different types of brands found within brand families:

The corporate brand

The corporate brand role depends on how prominent the company is in the brand proposition. It may include elements of social or business conduct, the relationship with suppliers and distribution channels and also be the employee brand (or internal-facing brand). Pure corporate brands are rare, but include companies such as General Electric and Philips, where all the products reflect the same brand as the company.

Family or umbrella brands

These brands support various products or services under the same name in different markets, such as Sony. Sometimes the umbrella brand may seem indistinguishable from a corporate brand; however, its role is different as it relates to the products and services rather than the activities of the company as a whole.

Individual brand

Here the brand may sit within the family with no obvious link to any of its siblings. For example, Ariel laundry products are owned by P&G but they have a strong, clearly identifiable, standalone presence within the brand family.

Modifier brands

These are product or service variants on a strong brand that will add a particular new attribute to the original brand. Modifier brands include Coke Zero as part of the Coca-Cola family, or the beer, Miller Lite.

Brand extensions

Brand extensions help a brand expand their audiences while innovating the existing brand. They build on the trust and loyalty of their audience and can also push the brand into more adventurous areas. For example, large supermarket chains now sell financial services under their own brand; fashion lines and clothing shops sell home interiors.

The ability to extend a brand will depend on how well it is established in the current market and how translatable the brand attributes are to new markets and opportunities.

Ways to extend the brand

Brands are becoming more innovative in the way that they extend products and services to enter new markets and attract new audiences.

This diagram offers a basic idea of the way that a brand may traditionally move beyond its core presence into new areas. New forms of media, emerging consumer tastes and diverse kinds of partnerships also open up further possibilities for brand extensions.

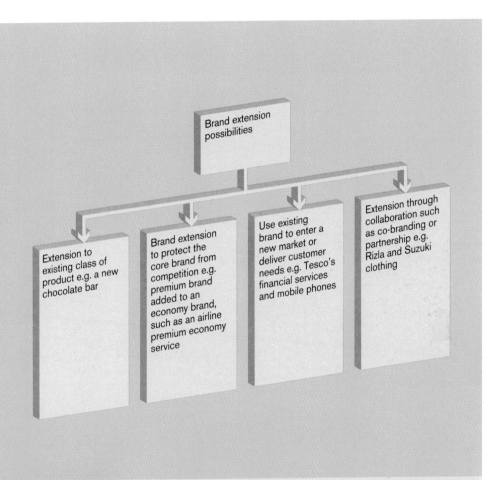

Brand extension possibilities

Extension to existing class of product e.g. a new chocolate bar

Brand extension to protect the core brand from competition e.g. premium brand added to an economy brand, such as an airline premium economy service

Use existing brand to enter a new market or deliver customer needs e.g. Tesco's financial services and mobile phones

Extension through collaboration such as co-branding or partnership e.g. Rizla and Suzuki clothing

Supermarket chain Tesco (far left) has added brand extensions to its portfolio that are as wide ranging as mobile phones and financial services (left). Each sub-brand carries the Tesco value proposition of affordability. The brand has also gone under the name 'Fresh & Easy' in the US market – this both localises the brand and reduces the risk to the parent brand if the new US market fails.

The brand development methodology

Brands do not come out of nowhere. They are meticulously researched, planned, strategised and marketed. Brand development should include business and product management as well as creative and marketing people.

The first step is to create a brand strategy. This should be detailed for any type of brand creation, whether refreshing an existing brand or extending the brand. It offers a central document to get people (including employees) to understand and buy into the direction of the brand, its values and purpose.

The brand framework and strategy

The brand strategy outlines a framework and direction for the brand. It is key in the brand development process and feeds into every part of the brand – into the creative process as well as into product and service development. Developing a brand strategy is usually supported by research. The strategy will detail the goals and rationale for the brand, providing both information about the market and its place in the market, including competitor insights. It will also cover audience insights and brand values and, from here, key messages about the brand can be developed. A strategy will identify where a brand will differentiate and feed into the creative development process.

Research and analysis

Research and analysis of the market, as well as of the brand's competitors and its audiences, are critical to any brand development. Many brand agencies will have specialist research teams (or freelancers) who focus on customer and social trends and insights. Research may be used at any stage in the brand process: from testing a brand name, to monitoring how people interact with a website or with a product on the supermarket shelf.

A **brand analysis** may include an internal review of the brand image, its heritage, its strengths and how they fit with the company's values. It may look at how the market is currently segmented in terms of features, price and performance. It may seek to uncover whether there are currently any gaps in the market that could define an opportunity – for example, new flavours, colours or packaging, or other areas such as more efficient energy consumption.

A **customer analysis** may address the major trends that affect the brand as well as the motivation behind customer buying and changing audience attitudes. Customer profiles are helpful here to ascertain the types of people that will buy into the brand, including their attitudes and needs, as well as in producing guidelines as to how to reach that audience.

A **competitor analysis** will map the relative brand image and awareness of the competitor; their perceived strengths and market strategies and also highlight any vulnerability in the competitor product or service, such as quality, price or functionality. It is also useful to look beyond direct competitors and view companies outside of the sector. This can help identify broader trends and gather ideas and influences for product and service design.

Translating research into action

It is critical that any research and analysis is interpreted in a way that is relevant and applicable to the brand's development. It sounds obvious but sometimes research is not used or applied. Research should feed into the brand planning process, the strategy and the creative development to the brand. A creative team will seek to gain an insight from the research – something that will give the brand an edge on which a creative campaign can be built.

Fashion insight

Successful fashion brands can offer some useful insight into branding and messaging. After all, they have to constantly stand out in an industry that often produces overlapping, competing products. Stores such as Urban Outfitters (US) or Topshop (UK) offer a particular shopping experience in addition to the clothes they sell.

Urban Outfitters is a US brand that initially successfully exported a bohemian, fun, 'hippy chick' look and evolved into a contemporary, funky store that is about clothing (of all kinds including designer labels), music and interiors.

Topshop transformed itself in the mid-1990s from a standard high-street retail chain into a fashionista 'mecca' frequented by everyone from girls of 15 (and their mothers!) through to supermodels. Its clothing ranges, some designed by UK model Kate Moss, alongside those of both up-and-coming and established fashion designers such as Celia Birtwell, have only added to its brand credibility – and sales.

The US brand Urban Outfitters has come a long way from its original 'hippy chick' image (top). Meanwhile, Topshop (above) continues to make waves with its Kate Moss collections. It opened a store in New York in 2009.

Brand positioning

A brand's position represents the brand's place in the market. It comes from developing the product or service image so that it occupies a distinct and valued place in the mind of the customer. The positioning will present a distinct proposition to the market that is in line with the brand's values and the needs and desires of the customer.

To determine a brand's position, it is essential to understand what the brand means to the customer as well as having a knowledge of the brand strategy. This then forms the brand's proposition – this is the central brand offer. The market proposition will be a combination of desired perceptions of quality, price and performance, coupled with an emotional connection to the style and tone of the brand, how people engage with it and why.

It is the strength and clarity of the proposition that drives the marketing strategy. This strategy will include ways in which to reach the audience, including where and how the brand is promoted and to whom. It will drive the brand experience. The brand may differentiate itself by a particular attribute – it may be fun or aspirational; it may differentiate itself by age group, location (such as the Internet) or means of access (exclusivity or membership).

Mobile phone brands

Mobile phone companies have become strong brands within the past five years as technology capabilities have increased and large brands continue to expand by buying up local operators in emerging markets. Yet mobile phone brands provide similar services to their customers. So how can a brand stand out beyond competing on price or deals to get customers on board?

In the UK, various mobile brands have taken a different brand position and vie for different parts of the market. For example, the 3 brand and T-Mobile have strong associations with the youth audience, Orange pushes its creative attributes while Vodafone tends to project a more functional image. O2, owned by Spain's Telefonica, associates itself with music – it transformed London's Millennium Dome building into a music venue called The O2, promotes special entry to events for its customers and also hosts the O2 Wireless Festival in the UK.

Any savvy brand has to look at all the touch points where the audience interacts with the brand – the total brand experience. In O2's case, the brand stands for being fresh and innovative and its goal is to always provide an enhanced experience for its audience – whether that's improving the packaging design, in-store experience or providing priority tickets to see a band at The O2.

Adrian Burton
Creative director / Lambie-Nairn

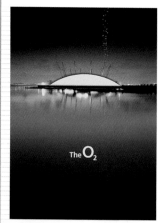

Mobile phone brand, O2, has successfully positioned itself as a brand linked to music since its purchase and rebrand of London's Millennium Dome – now called The O2 (above).

Distinguishing the brand

In markets where product and service differentiation is increasingly difficult, a brand proposition should encompass both the functional and emotional connection for the customer. Consumers, after all, increasingly expect brands to give them more than just a product or service, so connecting at both the functional and emotional level is important.

This means that products and features-led marketing strategies are only one element of what the brand has to offer. Brand values that are expressed through the brand experience bring in another dimension. In many cases, the customer will buy into brands that they associate with their own personal values.

Therefore, just as with human beings, the 'personality' of the brand matters! People will associate the brand with particular characteristics, such as a tone or a style, that may (or may not) resonate with their own personal tastes and desires.

Expressing innovation is also key to any brand – whether a consumer or business one. Clothing brand Benetton does this through provocative and, often, political advertising. Brands also now need visibility in the social networking space, rather than simply through traditional media forums (such as advertising).

Benetton's advertisements still manage to provoke and carry a social message. The 'victims' ad (above) shows a Tibetan monk with a member of the Chinese military – in surprising harmony.

The 'Africa works' ad (left) highlights entrepreneurial Africa to defy the general perception of Africa as a nation dependent on international aid money. It also flags up the Birima microcredit programme, which offers micro loans to enable people to set up small businesses.

Brand values

Brand values are a set of attributes that customers experience as the basis of the 'brand promise'. They give the brand personality and an emotional connection that drives trust and loyalty with the audience. Brand values are core to any brand – any deviation from a brand's values will run contrary to the original 'brand promise'.

Values are as important for employees of the company as they are for customers. Values should also be implicitly understood by anyone experiencing the brand – people should feel something when they come into contact with the brand. That said, a lot of companies like to communicate their values to their employees – usually expressed in a number of key words. But values are not a strapline or headline for a marketing campaign. Instead, they inform the behaviours of the company that will feed into the brand proposition and, in turn, will guide the creative direction of a company.

Contributing factors to brand personality

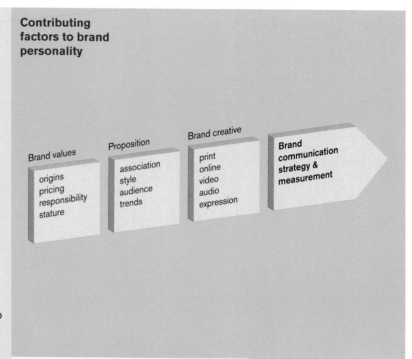

Brand values	Proposition	Brand creative	Brand communication strategy & measurement
origins pricing responsibility stature	association style audience trends	print online video audio expression	

Values in the brand personality

Brand values will be developed as part of the brand proposition and strategy. Is it critical that the values support the brand positioning and complement the brand's intended place and stature within the market? For example, a traditional English or American brand could play on values such as heritage, quality and national associations rather than attempt to be fun and funky.

Expressing the values

The challenge for many companies is how
to express and keep the momentum around
a brand's values as the company grows and
changes. This can be a particular challenge
for employees. Leadership here is key – the
company heads should demonstrate the
values of the company through action – but
values also need to come alive from the
bottom up.

Companies are starting to use their
contributions to communities or to a
'corporate responsibility' initiative as a way
to express a company's values and unite
employees around something tangible.
This may be a sponsorship or partnership
with a charity that offers employees the
opportunity to volunteer or fundraise. The
key for companies is to engage and inspire
employees around tangible actions rather
than words.

The BBC (right) is a publicly
funded UK organisation
renowned for authoritative
international journalism
and its strong values. The
BBC prides itself on being
independent, impartial and
honest.

The BBC's stakeholders
include the British public
who, as licence payers, are
listened to. There have been
incidents in which the 'Beeb'
has gone against its values
in broadcasting, which has
created a public uproar.

Case study
Pret A Manger

Pret A Manger is a chain of sandwich shops that opened in 1986 and now has around 150 shops, mostly in the UK, but also in New York and Hong Kong. The brand has a very distinct look and feel, employing dominant colours of deep crimson and stainless steel, with stars as a strong motif in the design. The language of the brand is simple and would appear to project an honest tone of voice that speaks directly to the customer.

Its brand values include freshness and quality, which ties in with Pret's central proposition that they are 'passionate about food'. The company promotes the fact that it has 'no nasties' in its food, and these values are carried across every aspect of the brand – from its packaging, to its clinical, stainless-steel environment, to in-store promotions, service levels and its community work – every evening leftover sandwiches are offered to homeless charities.

McDonald's acquired a stake in Pret in 2001, which was then sold to a private equity firm in 2008 (source: Brand Republic, 22 February, 2008). The McDonald's stake was well-publicised but seems not to have affected the values of the brand – or, ultimately, its sales.

'Just Made'
(and ready to take away)

Preservative free
Picnic
Summer menu 2008

★ PRET A MANGER® ★

⊨ BEFORE DAWN ⊨

Our sandwich and salad chefs make Pret sandwiches, baguettes and salads in-house during the day.
This is a huge challenge and totally essential to good quality.
Our fresh, natural ingredients are dropped off at each shop before dawn. We don't have a factory.
We hand make about 45 different products throughout the day. All of them straight from the shop's kitchen.

PASSION ★ FACT
No.26

Pret captured the market for fast and fresh sandwiches for the urban worker. Its values are core to the brand and are consistently promoted through the brand touchpoints (facing page and right).

⊨ HANDLE WITH CARE ⊨

Avocados are temperamental. When they are hard they are horrid. Our vegetable gardener Paul has a special avocado 'ripening room'. It's warm and filled with trays on which avocados are turned by hand (a bit like Champagne). Pret can use avocados because we make 'in store'. We don't sell 'long-life sandwiches'.

PASSION ★ FACT
No.40

⊨ SOFT AND SQUIDGY ⊨

We use only the freshest mozzarella cheese from Italy.
Soft, white, squidgy balls you find in proper cheese shops.
Mozzarella sausages, whilst a convenient shape and texture for sandwich making, simply aren't good enough.
We think the taste and texture of the real thing is worth all the extra effort.

PASSION ★ FACT
No.11

Developing the 'creative'

The creative teams are generally under the direction of the creative director or creative head. They will also work with a project director or account manager whose role it is to ensure that the project is delivered on time and to budget. Within a creative team, designers and copywriters are responsible for working together to develop creative concepts. Any strategy work and research that has been carried out should also be fed into the creative process and form part of the brief to the creative team.

A strong creative interpretation can sell a brand, giving it an identity that becomes inherent to the brand experience. Some brands prefer to have a consistent, creative experience across the different mediums – although it is always more exciting when brands allow for more creative experimentation, particularly in areas such as online design.

The creative brief

Any creative work should start with a good brief that details the objective of the work and the desired output. A brief aims to give the creative team direction, but not be so detailed as to constrain creativity. It will include information on the project such as the client's objective, what the campaign or brand development needs to achieve, and the current perceptions and performance of the brand. It should also detail the brand's audience, channels of delivery and timings.

The brief should provide enough detail to create some initial design concepts – this is usually pre-empted by a brainstorm with relevant members of the team, including designers and writers. It is also helpful to develop a narrative that can be a framework for a creative concept. At this stage, some agencies like to develop three initial conceptual routes to present to the client. One or two may then be later selected to take forward to full design.

Brand concepts

The strongest brand concepts always
develop visuals and words simultaneously,
with designers, writers and other team
members working together. Some branding
agencies have a tendency to focus more on
the visual design and brand 'look and feel' –
with words inserted into allocated spaces.
This is not ideal and is now an outdated way
of working.

The best way to approach concept creation
is to keep things flexible, allowing anyone
to contribute to the creative process and
so to come up with a great idea. In doing
so, it is worth considering how people will
be interacting with and experiencing the
brand – this is the 'human factors' or 'human
behaviours' approach which is often used
in web and product design. You can also
test this out on an audience. Ideas may
then be translated into a mix of words and
images, storyboards or scenarios – the
form it takes is flexible. A 'tone of voice' and
'look and feel' will underpin the visual and
verbal interpretation of the brand and are
fundamental to the overall brand experience.

The tone of voice will set the degree of
sophistication and accessibility, as well as
the tonal flavour of the brand (for example,
whether it is light-hearted or serious). It is
also used as a guideline for writing copy for
ongoing brand executions. The 'look and
feel' will include colours, imagery and the
visual expression of the brand, such as font,
layout and textures. Both the tone of voice
and look and feel are likely to be updated if
the brand changes (for example, if the brand
undergoes a revamp or 'refresh'). It is also
documented in brand guidelines to ensure
some degree of consistency (discussed
at the end of this chapter in 'Maintaining
the brand'). Any creative development
should always be checked against the
creative brief.

Executing the creative

The creative team will need to consider
the channels for communicating the brand.
Each channel has its own constraints – for
example, colours that work in print do not
necessarily translate onto the web.
Also, the style of language needs to be
adapted for different mediums – people
read in a different way online from how
they do in print. Each channel offers
opportunities to use different styles of
communication and messaging.

For print executions, the creative team has
to consider the context for the brand's
use to understand how it needs to be
reproduced at different sizes and colours.
For video or online, screen resolutions,
animation and audio components need
to be factored in. Each medium also
requires different skills from the creative
team – stretching from technical abilities
to specialist writing (such as scriptwriting)
and design. These skills may be provided by
freelancers.

Harvey Nichols is one of the leading high-end fashion department stores in the world. It first opened in 1813. It has always emphasised its creativity as an attribute – from its decadent window displays, to the shop layout, to the brands inside. US burlesque artiste, Dita Von Teese, endorses the Harvey Nichols brand (right).

In 1991, Harvey Nichols
used the strength of its
brand to open a food hall
(top) with its 'own label'
food products (above and
right), packaged in a similar
modern style to New York's
Dean & DeLuca deli.

Communicating the brand

Any brand revamp or 'refresh' – whether developing a brand or repositioning one – needs to be communicated well. However, this is an area that is so often considered as an add-on in many brand executions, rather than a fundamental part of the brand strategy. This is because so much focus is often directed into launching the brand or brand refresh, with less emphasis placed on how that brand will be communicated among employees or to other stakeholders.

How to communicate

Brand communications is about sustaining the brand in the market. The first six months of 'roll-out' is critical to the brand's success. People need to know what has changed and why it has been done. And any changes to the brand need to be communicated to all the brand's stakeholders, which includes external audiences – such as customers, investors and the press. One of the first areas of focus for any brand communications team should be the employees.

This means that any brand communications must be ongoing, rather than a 'quick hit' that happens with the launch. A new brand positioning needs to constantly be reinforced in people's minds, and messages must also be adapted to the different audiences. There is a huge range of tactics available to achieve this with both online and offline media. Essentially, the key is for companies to engage in conversation with their audiences, rather than dictate to them.

Engaging the employee audiences

Employees are the best communicators of any brand. Receive their buy-in and they can offer a loyalty that is as powerful as any supportive customer. Employees are an expression of the values of the brand – they are part of the brand's personality. Therefore, any brand launch, refresh or repositioning should involve employees at the outset. While this can make the brand process more complicated (by asking for more people's participation), it is an investment for the long term.

◀ Developing the
'creative'

▼ Communicating the
brand

▷ Maintaining the
brand

60–61

Communicating 'across'

Various tactics can be used to engage employees in new brand-related work. People need to feel involved and so communications must be two-way and not just from 'above', where bosses tell employees what is happening. There is scope for using various forms of communication, including poster campaigns, co-created campaigns, intranets, online radio and podcasts. Internal brand communications is a huge area of growth as companies realise the importance of employees to the brand.

Communicating for behaviour change

Chances are that a rebrand will seek to encourage some kind of behaviour change among audiences, towards the products and services that are being created. This may fundamentally involve asking the audience to see the brand from a different perspective; for example, if the brand has modernised – as heritage clothing brands Burberry and Aquascutum have – or has reinvented itself as many car brands do – for example, the Fiat 500, the Mini or the Volkswagen Beetle.

This can be even more difficult for brands that seek to change perceptions from a former low-end image to something of higher quality. The product must match higher-quality standards but so too must the branding. One example of this is Skoda, a car brand that was formerly associated with poor technology and design, but desperately wanted to reposition itself as a quality value brand under its new owner, Volkswagen. A redesign, new technology and some clever advertising encouraged customers to re-experience the product as a viable competitor in the lower mid-market.

Old-school brands can be successfully reinvented to modernise and appeal to a younger, less conservative audience. Aquascutum is a traditional British clothing brand that refers to itself as a 'quintessentially British luxury brand' with its roots in classic tailoring (above and left). The brand was reinvented in 2006, keeping its name, style and values but modernising its collection, tone of voice and shopping experience.

Communicating 'green' issues

Encouraging consumers to adopt new behaviours is particularly evident in areas such as the environment. Many large brands are now asking consumers to reconsider their perception of the brand, based around their 'sustainability' credentials. Brands such as UK retailers Marks & Spencer and Sainsbury's encourage people to question the source of their foods and buy more ethically produced goods. American giant, Walmart, has been instrumental in improving its supply chain.

Any communication to consumers that encourages more awareness around 'green' or environmental concerns needs to be matched by the behaviour of the company itself, as well as the product or service on offer. Over-exaggeration of 'green' claims, coupled with an inherent mistrust of companies, has led to audiences dismissing many claims as 'greenwash'.

However, product and service innovation to introduce more sustainable, responsible products for the environment is a huge potential growth area for brands. Challenges such as climate change are also critical business issues. Brands need to integrate 'green' into the central brand process to align it with their business practice, rather than treat these issues as a PR add-on, generated solely so that the brand is being seen to be doing the right thing.

Supermarkets are currently competing to demonstrate their 'green' and social credentials to their customers. Customers are concerned about the origin and sourcing of products, even though they may not purchase green products. Reducing the environmental impact of the way that things are packaged and transported can also reduce costs for the supermarket chains. UK supermarket, Tesco, displays its green credentials (above and left).

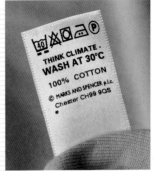

The British retail chain, Marks & Spencer (M&S), launched its 'Plan A' initiative to showcase its intentions around sustainability and social issues within a 100-point plan to its customers (above and left).

M&S provides an example of creative execution that runs right across the brand – affecting the quality of the product and its sourcing, the stores and the marketing. It has been a very successful positioning for M&S.

Maintaining the brand

Just as brands need to be constantly developed and evolved, the fundamental principles of the brand must also be maintained. This means ensuring that anyone who is working with the brand – from different departments within the company to different agencies – is executing it in a consistent manner.

This requires the 'buy-in' from the entire organisation to respect the brand guidelines and perimeters – it is not just within the remit of the brand managers. Through education and generating enthusiasm for the brand across the company – and therefore spreading the 'ownership' of the brand – the brand team can become more proactive, rather than simply policing the actions of the rest of the business. The creation of a brand manual or guidelines is essential to helping keep some consistency in the brand, and can be more flexible and practical as an electronic document.

Changing the rules of branding

The challenge for brand managers today is that the desire to 'control' the brand is more difficult in a world where online media and co-creation are becoming more central to branding. In this sense, the audiences are now taking more ownership of brands – and choosing to project them how they like. This can lead to some creative and fun interpretations of the brand.

But it also means that those responsible for the brand may have to be less afraid to let go and allow the brand to take on a life of its own. Just as the music industry creates popstars from the public, so are companies inviting participation from brand fans to help with advertising campaigns and creative concepts.

Clothing company Diesel created their 'Diesel Dreams' campaign, whereby people could make films for the Diesel brand. Even more traditional brands, such as Swarovski Crystal, allowed people to interpret its brand through film, music and photography. The campaign, run in 2008, was called 'The Three Graces', and used this Greek myth to unite the Swarowski brands within a simple narrative. Photographers, designers and actresses interpreted the three graces – joy, radiance and opulence – across leading magazines like *Vogue* and *Vanity Fair*. The Three Graces campaign can be found at <www.brand.swarowski.com>

◀ Communicating the
brand

▼ Maintaining the
brand

▷ Understanding the
brand audience

64–**65**

The brand manual

The brand manual is a document, folder or website that reflects the core elements of the brand. This includes the logo and its adaptations (including where and how it can be placed on the page), the tone of voice for the brand, its look and feel – including colours, tones and combinations, and brand elements such as imagery. A manual needs to explain how the brand can be adapted across various channels and medias, including screen adaptations and online versions of the brand. Other areas of exploration may include stationery, merchandising, campaign materials and brand 'extensions', such as furniture or vehicles.

Any manual should be designed to support the promotion of a company's brand and its products and services, rather than restrict them. Therefore, there needs to be some degree of freedom for the context in which the brand exists – such as cultural adaptations or allowing the brand to have a different kind of existence in the online space. It is important, therefore, that a manual is updated as necessary, with clear examples and rationale for the design limits and opportunities. Many companies use document management systems or pre-loaded templates designed to support the common documents routinely produced by the company.

Agency ownership

The external element to brand maintenance is very important, as many businesses provide sub-branding that can be used by partner and affiliate businesses, yet fail to give adequate consideration to its use and communication.

Branding agencies may act as the 'gatekeepers' for the brand, to ensure that both the company and its agencies comply with brand guidelines in spirit and execution. This enables the company to centralise the ongoing brand maintenance, while using the agency as a single point of contact for the brand execution. It also puts the agency in a strong position, as they will have ongoing input into the direction of the brand.

The availability of examples, reference artwork and tools in a convenient place can help support the brand, rather than hamper the business. Responsibility can also be delegated to those managing the various communications pieces to help speed up approvals of material.

The living brand

Brands are living entities and as business needs change, so too will the brand need to be refreshed and extended or refined. Any rationale for change should be well-communicated and involve people within the company in the brand development process – rather than dictating changes afterwards.

Any brand execution should be continually tested and checked against its values to make sure that the fundamental qualities that lie at the heart of the brand (and what makes it successful) are not altered or forgotten.

miCoach is a console in adidas stores that invites customers to test their core athletic skills through interactive touch-screen kiosk systems. Its aim is to help customers understand sport and improve personal fitness levels.

Customers can store personalised fitness reports and devise a sports training programme based on their test results. Beyond the store, customers can monitor their training from home through the website, and return to the store to repeat the tests and track their improvement.

miCoach also aims to offer a tangible brand experience that ties in with the adidas promise of 'enabling a better you'. It was created in collaboration with sports scientists, training consultants and retail and brand specialists.

A customer tries out miCoach in a Berlin store (left).

◀ Communicating the
brand

▼ Maintaining the
brand

▶ Understanding the
brand audience

66–67

To do

Create your own brand

Work on a scenario where you have been asked to create a new brand for the food and drink sector (or choose a different sector, if you prefer). Your role is to come up with an identity for the brand and a strategy to position and market the brand. You may want to consider the following:

→ First, think about the brands you like: what stands out? Why do you like those brands? Is there anything you dislike? What is distinct about the brand's personality?

→ Develop a marketing proposition: what does the market look like? Who are the competitors? Where do you want your brand to 'sit'? What are the aspirations for the brand? What kind of market research will you need? Who is the audience?

→ What will be the brand's key values? For example, will the materials be sustainable? Will it offer any distinct ingredients or design value?

→ Develop the creative for the brand: what will it look like? What will it be called? How will it be packaged?

→ Can you describe the brand in four or five words?

→ Think about the business side of the product: how will the product be distributed? How can it stand out on the supermarket shelf?

The changing brand audience

Understanding the brand audience

Central to the brand process is to understand the brand's audience. It sounds simple, but like people, brands grow and transform. There was a time when brands communicated to their audiences in a one-sided manner. The audience could be divided into simple categories that described a person's wants and consumer needs based on their age, profession, marital status and social class. Television, billboards or direct mail 'spoke' to those people and they, in turn, bought the product. Things were less complex then.

Consistency and coherency are key when you need to talk to different audiences – like youth or business – each must be spoken to individually ... never take a broad-brushed approach for a brand as you lose the relevance.

Adrian Burton
Creative director / Lambie-Nairn

◀ Maintaining the
brand

▼ Understanding the
brand audience

▷ Audience attitudes and
social shifts

70–71

The changing audience

Some decades later, the world has moved on. Audiences have changed, diversified and segmented, just as the means and mediums to reach them have broadened. People are no longer necessarily loyal to one brand – they may be willing to try many – but they will buy into those brands that they identify with and associate as matching their own values. New channels and methods of communication mean that people now engage with brands in a different way – with less time, higher expectations and more knowledge. These shifts have blurred the boundaries of audience behaviour, making it simpler to define a brand's audience by their attitudes, values and needs rather than their age or social class.

The segmented audience

Just as audiences have merged and overlapped, they have also segmented. Brands now have a spectrum of people to target. Rather than projecting a brand in a different way to different people, brands need to remain clear and relevant in their audience communication, through their tone, style and behaviour, as well as in the experience offered to the audience. At the same time, consumers want to be spoken to at an individual level.

This means that it is important for a brand to be consistent and coherent when talking to different audiences – yet each audience must also be spoken to individually. Creatively, therefore, an agency may work on a number of different creative ideas or executions at any one time for a client project; for example, implementing a different creative idea for a youth audience from that for a business audience.

The new audience context

The challenges lie in trying to understand how audiences now interact with brands in rapidly evolving environments. Customisation through technology is helping brands to target communications at an individual level. The style of brand communication is also changing as brands shift from a one-sided 'us-to-them' delivery, to a two-way conversation with their audiences. This is sometimes taken further with companies asking for active input and participation from customers, particularly in the online space. This can range from encouraging feedback on services to co-creating products.

Creating trust and loyalty

At the heart of any brand engagement is the marketer's desire to inspire loyalty and trust among its audiences, old or new. Loyalty and trust can easily be lost if the audience has a negative experience of the brand such as poor service or bad press. Once lost, trust is hard to rebuild.

Brands consequently use many ways in which to encourage loyalty among customers. Loyalty schemes, such as air miles or store cards, where points are accumulated through purchasing, are ways of enticing customers to return for repeat purchases. Some brands, such as those that are associated with a country's heritage – Ford Motors, the UK's Royal Mail or a national airline, for example – court an ingrained trust in the brand because their identity is deeply rooted in the national psyche. In Royal Mail's case, its name links itself to the British public and history with its royal association. However, deregulation and increasing competition have taken their toll on a postal service that struggles with 21st century service expectations and competes with new technology. Heritage associations can also make it difficult for a brand to promote any radical change; attempts at which may lay the brand open to public scrutiny and criticism.

Building trust in a brand must run deeper than using tactics such as customer incentives and marketing. A brand must stay true to its core values and not change these to attract new audiences or markets. They must also continuously reflect these values through their products, services and actions. Importantly, they must deliver on their brand promise, whether to a business audience (B2B), consumer audience (B2C) or employee audience. An open dialogue with audiences is both sensible and crucial.

☐ I'd like a more reliable, less expensive service, please.

☐ No way, I insist on paying more for a service that isn't quite as good.

Independent research proves Royal Mail's 9.00am Special Delivery service is more reliable than DHL, TNT, Business Post and City Link. And it's still less than half the price of any of them. So to save money and get a better service, go to www.royalmail.com/specialdelivery, telephone 08457 950 950, or visit your local Post Office® branch.

Royal Mail
specialdelivery®

9AM GUARANTEED* FROM JUST £9.35

Royal Mail

with us it's personal®

*Guaranteed by 9am or your money back. Service available to 99% of UK addresses. Research conducted by Research International 2006. Royal Mail, Royal Mail Special Delivery, Royal Mail Special Delivery logo, Royal Mail with us it's personal, the cruciform and the colour red are registered trademarks of Royal Mail Group Ltd. All Rights Reserved. Post Office is a registered trade mark of Post Office Ltd.

Royal Mail is the UK's main postal service with a history of over 360 years (above and left). It is indicative of a 'heritage brand' – one that has a close association with a country's history and its people.

◄ Maintaining the
brand

▼ **Understanding the
brand audience**

▷ Audience attitudes and
social shifts

72–**73**

We are very promiscuous as a brand audience. Our loyalties change. Traditionally we were 'buying into' the brand; now we can decode all this and emotional engagement on its own is not enough. Audiences want a more practical relationship with brands, where reality and functionality matter.

Robert Jones
Wolff Olins

Audience attitudes and social shifts

Today's brand audience is able to access information more quickly than ever before. They have greater choice in products than any previous generation has had. They are more discerning, savvier and better connected than generations of the past. They are able to voice their opinions online or elsewhere, to tell brands what they think and to choose from any competitor if one brand fails to meet their expectations.

Audience expectations

As consumers, we often have an erratic relationship with brands. Despite buying into brands, many people also mistrust the companies behind them. People are often sceptical of company motives and few trust that business leaders (the CEOs) will tell the truth. We also have higher expectations of companies than we place on ourselves: a survey by researchers Ipsos MORI in 2008 found that people expect brands to behave responsibly in areas such as the environment, even if the individual does nothing.

This mix of emotions and lack of trust can directly impact on a brand and its reputation. Consumers now expect a certain degree of integrity from the products and services that they buy into, and want the experience to meet with their own expectations and values. Brands are responding in various ways, such as: attempting to be more transparent about the business behind the brand; by promoting a CEO blog; or by offering corporate site forums to manage feedback on issues, such as Shell's 'Tell Shell'. Any attempts at 'openness', however, must be followed by action.

Jenny Dawkins, Head of corporate responsibility and research at Ipsos MORI, UK, claims that: 'Recent years have seen rising expectations of business to behave responsibly towards society and the environment, both among consumers and other stakeholder groups. A company will have to monitor stakeholder expectations and formulate robust responses to these demands if it is to be successful in the future'.

◀ Understanding the
brand audience

▼ Audience attitudes and
social shifts

▷ Developing brands for
audience 'types'

74–75

Brands as a barometer of personal beliefs

In this new brand context, a brand's values and what it contributes to a person's belief system has become the decisive choice factor for many. This applies to what car people drive, what clothes they wear, what food they eat. Price and location also matter, but values can be the differentiator for the discerning consumer or for one making a choice between similarly priced brands. Those values can be anything from demonstrating wealth and being part of a particular elite class – such as when purchasing the latest Audi convertible – to demonstrating more morally based buying choices, such as choosing a 'green', environmentally conscious brand such as the Toyota Prius.

Brands must be in tune with these changes in society as well as with wider cultural currents. The current 'ethical' stance in Western Europe is for brands to be more environmentally responsive, though this is not yet necessarily evident in newer consumer markets such as those of the Ukraine, China or India. Brands in these emergent consumer markets are often associated with a status and wealth and so environmental concerns may be secondary or not considered at all. Likewise, in tougher economic times, consumers may make less discerning choices regarding quality or ethics, and simply buy on price.

Today's brands exist in a new environment that poses challenges to marketers. The emergence of social media, environmental and social responsibility and segmented audiences (such as the super-rich, those in developing countries or young teenagers), have created more complex environments for brands, which offer opportunities for brands to move to new, different levels of engagement, or to lead in a particular area.

The Toyota Prius is one of Toyota's most well-known car brands and is considered to be a leader in ecologically friendly cars (above and left). Its success has led to a perception of Toyota as a 'green' brand.

Audience 'self-actualisation'

Audiences in the West often seek another dimension from brands that fulfils something in themselves as a person – they want brands that make them feel better or may reflect their own values. This '**Self-actualisation**' is the upper level represented by Abraham Maslow's 'Hierarchy of needs' (1943).

But different societies respond to brands in different ways. Interbrand's Jonathan Chajet points out that consumers in China seek brands to reflect their status (the same could be said of the Indian middle classes), where the needs of a superior (a boss or someone older) matter before the individual. This is represented by Maslow's '**Esteem**' level.

Brands are even relevant to those who earn just above the poverty level. Studies have shown that people will often purchase a television or other consumer item before they have access to other basic, **Physiological** needs (such as running water). This may be because purchasing goods offers a degree of control to the person, while basic needs may be dependent on government provision. Targeting people at the poorer level of developing societies is often referred to as 'the bottom of the pyramid' (coined from Prahalad) – the notion being that these people represent the future middle classes and therefore signify a viable consumer market.

Maslow's hierarchy of needs

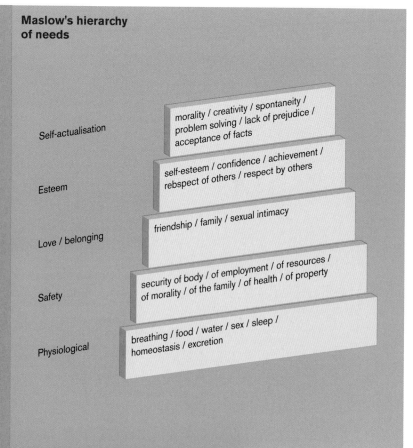

Self-actualisation — morality / creativity / spontaneity / problem solving / lack of prejudice / acceptance of facts

Esteem — self-esteem / confidence / achievement / rebspect of others / respect by others

Love / belonging — friendship / family / sexual intimacy

Safety — security of body / of employment / of resources / of morality / of the family / of health / of property

Physiological — breathing / food / water / sex / sleep / homeostasis / excretion

◀ Understanding the
brand audience

▼ **Audience attitudes and
social shifts**

▷ Developing brands for
audience 'types'

76–77

Case study
Monocle

Monocle started as a magazine for the sophisticated international jetsetter, who wanted to be informed of both international issues as well as the latest in design. It is slowly developing into a trendy, luxury brand by introducing products for this certain type of readership, that are co-created with top designers under the Monocle brand. This includes a Monocle fragrance from Comme des Garçons, Monocle-branded travel goods and designer furniture.

The magazine, *Monocle*, launched in 2007, and shown are some of its magazine covers (above and left). Monocle also has its own shopping range, including a bicycle (top left) and fragrance (top) designed for Monocle by Comme des Garçons, called Scent One: Hinoki.

Developing brands for audience 'types'

The buying power of individuals has increased as parts of society have become more affluent. Couple this with an increasingly fragmented media, spanning endless TV channels, magazines, online media and forms of advertising, and it is easy to see how brand audiences have become much more segmented, forming their own individual communities and associations.

Dividing audiences into segments can help identify a larger group of people with similar tastes. It has spawned a range of distinct audience 'types'. A brand may offer a key service or product for that audience and then extend the range. This audience segmentation may lead brands to adopt a variety of means to catch the customer's attention – from mainstream advertising to forms of digital advertising and ambient media.

Emergent markets and the creation of new audiences

New lucrative, segmented markets include the 'mass exclusive' audience, which has been created to offer services for an increasingly affluent group of people. The boutique hotel, private members' clubs and premium economy on airlines all cater for this market. Another example is the 'Mums' market – particularly featuring older and more affluent mums – that in recent years has driven up the sales of organic food for children.

'Tween' brands are another growth segment, targeting young girls aged 8–12 years old, who do not consider themselves children anymore and who may share similar interests in celebrities, fashion and make-up. It was popularised by the success of the Olsen twins and the younger Britney Spears in the late 1990s. In the US, it is estimated that 'tweens' spend over US $10 billion every year on themselves, with their parents spending over US $175 billion. The market is estimated to grow at 15 per cent each year (according to figures supplied by the Kellogg School of Management).

Targeting segmented audiences may sound simpler than trying to be a large brand serving different markets. This segmentation can bring a deeper brand experience to a given particular audience by serving only that audience – and so people are prepared to experiment with that brand if it introduces other products and services.

◁ Audience attitudes and
social shifts

▼ Developing brands for
audience 'types'

▷ Brands, ethics and
responsibility

78–79

Case study
Stardoll

Stardoll is an online brand created for the 'tween' and teenage market. It is a website for girls to dress up and 'makeover' celebrities, with celebrity dolls, clothes and accessories online. It currently has nearly 30 million members (in April 2009) from over 200 countries. The site makes money from payments by users as well as marketing partnerships with fashion, retail and media brands.

The new 'tween' audience courts some controversy, as an obvious concern is that marketing to these young girls encourages them to buy into brands, make-up, clothes and celebrity culture. Yet, it also offers a community for these girls, for whom brands and technology are simply part of everyday life.

Girls in the 'tween' market do not differentiate between the online world and offline. They will ask for new labels on the site that they know from everyday life, so we add them in – like the DKNY new season wardrobe. We've extended the website by listening to what our members want.

Matt Palmer
Managing director / Stardoll

Stardoll (above) is an online community for girls who like to go shopping and love dressing up. Members of the website create a MeDoll avatar that they can dress up, shop for, and whose room they can decorate.

Case study
Gaydar

Gaydar.co.uk was first set up as an online personal dating service for the gay community in 1999 – when online dating was in its infancy. The brand has successfully extended its presence both online and offline, as well as internationally, to offer other services for the gay community.

Its online brand extensions include GaydarGirls, GaydarRadio and GaydarNation, an online lifestyle magazine with news, events and gossip. Offline, the brand has opened up nightclubs and bars, as well as mobile services.

People in the gay community want brands that understand their lifestyle and needs. Gaydar started when online dating was in its infancy. We're unusual in that we have built the brand from the online world to the offline. We can do that because we are a trusted brand within the gay community and we know what our specific market wants.

Mark Mangla
Creative director / Gaydar

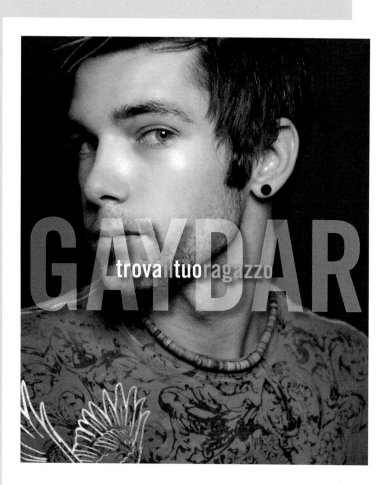

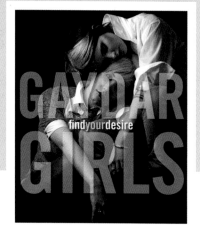

ilmiglioresitodiannuncipersonaligay

Gaydar offers locally tailored content such as its Italian site, Gaydar.it (above). GaydarGirls is an online dating site for gay women (left).

◁ Audience attitudes and
social shifts

▼ Developing brands for
audience 'types'

▷ Brands, ethics and
responsibility

80–81

To do

Imagine this scenario ...

You have been working on a rebrand for a large multinational company. The client asks you to create a campaign that will help communicate the rebrand to employees and also engage them – to feel proud and endorse the new brand. Your role is to provide ideas and concepts for the employee campaign. Select a brand that has recently been updated and consider the following:

→ What kind of strategy can be put in place during the rebrand process to involve employees? Think about the way companies often 'speak' to their own employees. What would you do differently?

→ Consider trends in branding, such as encouraging participation through online media or allowing people to create their own services. Could these tactics be used among employees to make the rebrand fun?

→ What will be the key messages to the employees?

→ What kind of communication material will you develop to make employees aware of the rebrand and your messages?

→ Can you involve any partner companies or charities in the rebrand?

Brands, ethics and responsibility

In the past decade, society – particularly in the Western world – has become increasingly concerned about ethics and sustainability. This new wave of social and environmental consciousness no longer resides solely with a niche audience of 'eco-warriors' or activists; it is fast becoming mainstream across society, particularly as knowledge of issues such as climate change become widespread. This is one of the leading issues for brands today. It is directly impacting on the way that brands communicate with their 'stakeholders' – that is, those who are impacted by the actions of the company or who experience the brand.

Taking a stand – to stand out

Some brands are adopting an ethical approach as a brand differentiator – as a way to make products stand out from competitors on the supermarket shelf, particularly by collaborating with charities or by campaigning for a social or an environmental purpose. For example, Ariel's 'Do a good turn' campaign promotes energy-saving washing at 30°C (<www.doagoodturn.co.uk>) which is linked to its offline product campaigns. Other brands are using sustainability concerns as an opportunity to innovate in product design by introducing 'green' products.

Younger companies, such as clothing manufacturers Howies and American Apparel, or water product 'One', promote an 'ethical' brand to their customers in different ways. All have broad audience appeal rather than accessing only those concerned about ethics. These younger, more flexible brands have successfully created a loyal following – and offer a choice to the 'conscious consumer' that has influenced the larger global brands.

American Apparel is a growing casual brand with an ethical bent, that has moved into the mainstream, expanding its shops outside of the US (far right and below).

Social values and ethics remain at the heart of the brand, including immigration rights (right). While this is not necessarily visible in the shopping experience, it adds another dimension to the brand story.

AMERICAN APPAREL ON IMMIGRATION

Made in USA

Crafted with pride in Los Angeles, California.

American Apparel®

The Figure Skater Dress

American Apparel®

Ariel's 'turn to 30' campaign encourages people to wash their clothes at 30°C or below (right). Ariel has deliberately targeted the mainstream consumer, rather than a niche, eco-conscious consumer.

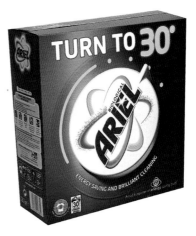

Political conscience or greenwash?

The connection between ethical issues and big brands can create an uneasy association. Some academics and business people believe that it is not the role of brands – or the companies in the background – to relieve social ills. The wave of ethical initiatives by large brands is also often met with scepticism by consumers. Many consumers accuse brands of 'greenwash' – when the good deeds done by a single campaign or promotion is not reflected across the whole company or brand lines. If a brand is to adopt any element of sustainability, then that must be acted upon and reflected across the whole company, from its operations to its communications.

However, it is likely that brands will continue to integrate social and environmental concerns into product and service ranges, as well as into the business practice behind the brands. After all, it presents a great opportunity for brands to innovate in areas such as green products and services. From an audience perspective, issues such as climate change and poverty will not disappear and brands that fail to engage with these issues will be in danger of being perceived as outdated or uncaring. Brands now have to demonstrate greater transparency and more responsible behaviour. The key is to embrace this in a true, authentic manner that is ingrained throughout the business before it is communicated.

Howies is an ethical, but mainstream brand with a loyal following. Its clothes are made from sustainable sources. Howies' visual style promotes the idea of freedom – without having to include the logo as a visual identity (above and facing page).

howies®

Social media chatter

The growth of online communities and chatter, particularly on the blogs, can impact brands in both positive and negative ways. Brands that have felt the bite of social banter include Kryptonite Locks, a lock company that failed to mitigate the online dialogue, on forums and blogs, about one of its products that could be broken into. The story then reached the mainstream press and the company was forced to act after its share price dropped. Increasingly, companies are using the online chatter to their advantage.

Charities such as Oxfam and Greenpeace have long used online communications to campaign for change. One of Greenpeace's more popular campaigns is its 'Green my Apple' campaign – a spoof Apple website where people have created posters and videos to encourage Apple to be more 'green' in its products.

Green my Apple.

www.greenmyapple.org

Greenpeace started a very creative online campaign in 2006 to encourage Apple to make its products more 'green' (top). Apple fans were asked to submit green designs for the iPod; one entry is shown here (left).

Case study
Peugeot

Car manufacturers constantly battle to be distinctive from competitors through advertising, design and creative marketing. For the past five years, Peugeot has run its design competition to encourage young designers from all over the world to design a car for Peugeot based around a theme. There is an emphasis on mobility that works for people without damaging the environment.

The idea helps boost the Peugeot brand while attracting young talent. The fifth competition in 2008 attracted over 2,500 entries from 95 different nationalities. Projects were shortlisted by a jury and then the press and public were able to vote for the final ten on the shortlist. A winning concept is made into a scale model concept car, with the opportunity to work with the Peugeot design team to build the car.

The Peugeot design competition is a leading example of 'co-creation' where the public participate in creating new designs, products or concepts for companies and have a say in which is best. Engagement with customers is increasingly being used among brands, and if executed in a clever way, can boost the profile of the brand, offer insight from customers, tap into outside talent and add a fun dimension to the brand.

MIHAI PANAITESCU'S LIFE SIZE MODEL OF 'FLUX'.
THE 2007 WINNER OF THE 4TH PEUGEOT DESIGN COMPETITION

For more information and additional pictures visit www.peugeotpress.co.uk or call the Press Office on 024 7688 4212

09/2007 © Copyright Peugeot Motor Company PLC, reproduction free for editorial use only

THE PEUGEOT RC HYbrid4 CONCEPT
For more information and additional pictures visit www.peugeotpress.co.uk or call the Press Office on 024 7688 4212
11/2008 © Copyright Peugeot Motor Company PLC, reproduction free for editorial use only

The Peugeot Design Competition is run every year to attract young design talent from around the world. The 'concept cars' are life-size scale models of previous winners (top and left).

Case study
Avaaz

Avaaz is a website that has created a global web movement of 3.3 million members (April 2009) who petition online for political change around specific issues. Set up in January 2007, it is used to influence international politics and raise awareness of serious social, political and environmental issues.

Avaaz cleverly uses its online campaigns to encourage people to take action on specific days in events that tie in with the online protests. Its broad campaign remit is also unusual, which may account for its high membership numbers (other activists' groups tend to focus on one key issue or area of engagement).

Online activism is becoming an increasingly popular way of petitioning and campaigning, including targeting corporations and brands.

AVAAZ.ORG

Set up in 2007, Avaaz means 'voice' in some languages. It has members from every nation in the world (above). It actively campaigns and lobbies on a range of human rights and environmental issues, from lobbying the Burmese junta to free its democratic leader, Aung San Suu Kyi, to lobbying the World Health Organisation to regulate farms that have enabled the spread of swine flu.

Case study
Wikipedia

Wikipedia is one of the most well-known co-creation sites, on which people add their own encyclopedia entries. At times, the accuracy of entries has been questioned, but a study by the scientific journal *Nature* in 2005 concluded that the entries were as accurate as *Encyclopædia Britannica*.

The term 'wiki' has come to mean a new online model in which people are able to contribute to a collection of web pages that are available for free. It is used to build external sites, such as Wikipedia, as well as for company intranets. Effectively, it is similar to the 'open source' model, where people are able to contribute to the building of a useful online resource, product or service.

Wikipedia is the online encyclopædia that was set up in 2001. Anyone is able to contribute and edit entries, and any disputed content can be removed. The Wikipedia logos are shown here (above and right).

Employee audiences

Employees are a core part of any brand. They are a central expression of the brand because they connect the company to the outside world, as representatives of the company. Brand agencies will often work on projects to help communicate any changes or develop the brand to employees. 'Employee engagement' has also become a growth area as bosses seek new ways in which to motivate and engage employees, to inspire them and make them more productive.

Strong employee values within a company are key to internal branding. Companies often talk about employees 'living the brand' to create a consistent experience of the brand. The reality is that a company's values should be embedded in the company's culture and company employees are the clearest expression of the brand values. This is evident in companies with strong cultures – from big brands such as Microsoft and Google to eco-brands like Patagonia.

Internal branding

An important audience for brands – and just as critical as its customers – is its employees. These employees are not only representatives of the brand but can be avid promoters – or critics – of the company that they work for. Branding inside organisations – particularly within companies – runs wide and deep. Over the past decade, organisations have become more sophisticated at internal branding as a way to inspire and engage employees, unite people across the company and attract 'talent'.

The growth in internal branding is significant as an increasing number of companies offer services rather than 'things'. The quality of that service can differentiate a company from its competitors, and that requires employee commitment and belief in the brand. After all, contact with an employee is often the first experience of a brand (for example, in a shop or hotel). Yet, communicating effectively to employees is quite different from communicating to customers, as employees have different needs and expectations of the brand from customers.

Leadership is a starting point for an organisation's branding. Strong leadership can help turn a brand around, changing perceptions both within and outside the company: Steve Jobs at Apple or Richard Branson at Virgin offer examples of strong characters at the helm. Leadership, however, should not just come from the top of the company: brand culture is also created by employees and internal branding must involve people at all levels of the company.

Case study
TNT

Internal brands can be used as a device to communicate a campaign or particular part of the organisation. For example, mail and express company TNT created a brand called 'Moving the World' for its partnership with the World Food Programme (WFP) – a partnership that played a role in uniting TNT's global employees around volunteering and fundraising for the WFP.

People within TNT can volunteer to work for three months with WFP and become 'storytellers' for the partnership. Employees also fundraise for WFP. TNT has since been recognised as a top European employer by *Fortune* magazine and the partnership has huge awareness within the company. The branding of corporate responsibility initiatives as separate brand identities within companies is a current trend.

TNT volunteers work with WFP's School Feeding Programme (above). TNT also runs a 'Colour the World' competition for school children to raise awareness of global child poverty and the work of the WFP (below).

Branding techniques

Techniques to diversify the brand

Collaboration among brands has developed significantly in the past decade, as brands have joined forces to offer consumers more choice, extend their portfolios or seek to differentiate their own brand in a new way. Partnering among brands offers opportunities to diversify and leverage the credibility of one brand against the other. It also enables the companies behind the brands to share knowledge and technologies. In doing so, the alliance or partnership may create a new product or market for the customer, by giving them something that was never there before. Collaboration can also be used by a brand to enter new sectors outside of that brand's core competency.

Cigarette rolling-paper brand, Rizla, teams up with car manufacturer, Suzuki, for the MotoGP (above). The partnership adds a new dimension to both brands, through joint credibility and by offering new products and services to the public, such as a range of biker clothing.

Unusual partnerships

The best collaborations will delight the consumer through unusual partnerships. For example, Rizla (which makes cigarette rolling paper) and automobile and motorbike manufacturer, Suzuki, joined forces to create a range of clothes for motorbike riders. On the one hand, this is a natural extension of the two brands' co-sponsorship of the British Superbike team – the key players in UK motorbike racing. On the other hand, it is an unusual joint product association – moving Rizla away from the stereotypical association of old men smoking roll-ups into a world of speed, leathers and superbikes instead; while also shifting the image of Suzuki bikes into a 'cool' status when combined with the clothes.

These kinds of collaborations indicate that the brands involved in such product alliances are effectively mutually endorsing each other's status and value as a brand – much like a partnership within a couple. It also reinforces the promotion of each partner's own product or service, with the goal of ensuring a profitable outcome for both parties.

Collaborative benefits

For companies, collaboration can also offer a brand a vehicle to test new markets and audiences, with limited damage to the brand if things don't work out. A collaboration may be viewed as experimental by consumers and the brands involved taking a risk – thus failure to make it work may be seen more as a short-term hiccup rather than leaving a long-term negative impression of a given brand.

For the customer, collaborations between brands that work have the potential to deepen the brand experience. For example, the Apple iPod and Nike association offers a new convenient product for runners (with an iPod designed for running) and also introduces the Apple brand to an audience that may not have previously considered buying an iPod.

Case study
Apple and Nike iPod

In 2006, Apple and Nike teamed up to produce the Nike + iPod Sport Kit. The partnership has been clever from a marketing collaboration stance: the companies took two technologies with a common audience – that of runners – and used their skills to combine shoe design with a mobile music experience. The Nike + iPod is a sensor that is promoted as a personal trainer, tracking statistics such as distance, pace and calories from a Nike+ running shoe and onto an iPod nano screen via wireless technology and through the iPod's computational abilities.

The product is a simple but brilliant idea for runners and gym-goers who were already using the two products – and for others who may be encouraged to buy the product for its technological capabilities. For Apple, it shows that the iPod is more than a music machine; for Nike, it enhances the running experience and therefore their brand. One of the strengths of the product has been the NikePlus social networking community which connects Nike + iPod runners. The aim is to better the individual's performance by setting goals and creating an international network of runners who challenge and compete with each other. For Nike, the product can also be developed based on their own customer input.

The partnership represents a mutual endorsement of each other's brands; the premier brand position of each partner ensured instant profile and credibility for the product. However, from a reputational standpoint, Nike seems to have had a head start. Some of Apple's loyal fanbase questioned the partnership in terms of the values that each company is commonly associated with. While both are innovative leading brands, Nike's image is still tarnished by its child labour scandals in the mid-1990s (although the company now leads its sector in supply chain standards).

This could potentially have had a negative impact on Apple's brand, which represents creative expression.

The partnership succeeded where others have failed (for example, Nike's former collaboration with Philips Electronics was not generally considered a success). It also emphasises each individual brand proposition – of ease of use as well as of technical and design leadership. And sales have been high: within months, Nike had reported an increase in its profits due to sales of the joint product as well as converting runners from other shoe brands. The product can easily be replicated across other areas of sport – a fairly easy step for both companies.

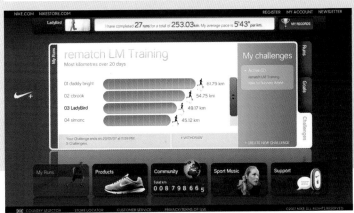

The Nike + iPod Sport Kit is a product developed by both Apple and Nike to fulfil the role of a personal trainer (above). It is a wireless sensor and receiver that fits in a Nike+ shoe to connect to an iPod nano or iPod touch to track the runner's performance. Runners can also connect and compete around the world through the community on the NikePlus website (left).

Forms of collaboration

There are many techniques that can be used to diversify a brand and extend its reach. Some, such as sponsorship or co-branding, are common techniques that have become more innovative in recent years. Others, such as online collaboration, are more recent developments.

The past decade has seen a huge increase in celebrity endorsement and brand collaboration – including celebrities introducing their 'own brand' ranges. Celebrity endorsement will often aim to make the product or service more visible or credible – and lead to increased sales by enhancing its reputation and image. It can also offer shoppers a new range of goods while extending the brand affiliation between the company and its consumers. In other cases, the joining of two strong brands can boost a new product or service – if the idea is good enough. Alternatively, the presence of an 'endorser' brand can be used to create new product ranges.

This section outlines some basic forms of collaboration.

Sponsorship

Sponsorship is perhaps the most traditional approach of collaboration (for example, sponsoring festivals) where a brand will pay a sum for the presence of its logo and wares. It is closely related to co-branding, as elements of the experience are similar. However, sponsorship tends to be an extension of advertising space rather than the joint venturing aspect of most co-branding activities. Therefore, the benefits of the relationship can be harder to measure – much depends on the level of visibility that the sponsor will receive, combined with the reputation of the event, person or product (such as a TV show) that is sponsored.

Sponsorship is an area of branding that has undergone huge growth in recent years and appears to know no boundaries. It is now common on television shows, at music festivals and most noticeably in sport, where brands battle to discover the up-and-coming athletes of the future. Sponsorship is also entering more traditional institutions such as academia and schools. This raises ethical concerns for many people, particularly if partnerships are chosen on the basis of cash contributions rather than brand association.

Co-branding

In a simple co-brand arrangement, each brand has equal billing and transfers the brand experience to the co-brand partnership. Good examples of this are co-branding of credit cards, such as the British Airways or Virgin Atlantic American Express cards; in both, the premium nature of the airlines matches the aspirational nature of American Express. Their joint heritage in travel reinforces the alliance and offers equal credibility, benefiting the customer with joint concierge benefits. The co-branding additionally encourages spending on the cards to collect air points!

A co-brand normally has a direct financial relationship, such as sharing the cost of promotion to build a market. The specific form of the co-branded partnership can take many forms and behind-the-scenes deals may not be evident to the consumer. For example, the airlines KLM and Air France project an equal balance between the brands, but KLM actually has the dominant share of the partnership. The degree of tight coupling between the companies will vary depending on the objective of the relationship, but may extend to a formal business joint venture.

Co-branding offers opportunities for brands to be creative in product and service development, particularly when the coupling is unlikely and works across different sectors; as when cosmetics company, Shiseido, and Coca-Cola launched a cosmetics and beverage range in Japan. A more pronounced relationship was struck up when electronics company, Sony, and mobile technology company, Ericsson, got together to create mobile phones. As joint partners, they could reduce the cost of both development and marketing in an increasingly fast-paced, competitive market.

Endorser brands

Endorser brands are brands that provide credibility to a dominant market brand when innovating in new areas. This can help the dominant brand gain access to new markets where a shift in perception may be needed – such as if a food range wants to enter the organic or healthy eating market. For example, Weight Watchers products by Heinz effectively reposition the Heinz brand in an increasingly health-conscious market. Weight Watchers, in return, provides the credibility for managing diets. Endorsements from well-known ethical brands are starting to become more ubiquitous as large brands enter the eco-conscious market.

Endorsements also come in the form of celebrity endorsement – a very common tactic today where celebrities will be the face of a particular brand. The association is obviously aimed at selling more products via the 'cool' factor or glamour of the celebrity. This is a tactic long-used by sports brands – Michael Jordan and Nike's relationship is perhaps one of the most well-known – and is now frequently used to promote jewellery and perfumes. For example, George Clooney and Daniel Craig endorse Omega watches, and Police sunglasses formerly gained cool credibility through the endorsement of David Beckham.

UK actor, Daniel Craig, endorses Omega watches (top) as James Bond 007 (above). Celebrity endorsements of high-end brands are a commonly used strategy to attract attention and customers.

Sainsbury's

Try something new today

Celebrity chef, Jamie Oliver (left), is the face of UK supermarket chain, Sainsbury's. Oliver has linked his chef skills to many social causes, including encouraging people – especially kids – to eat well.

His 'school dinners' campaign challenged the UK government to improve the quality of school meals, by replacing junk food with nutritious meals and foods presented in a different way, simply cooked and with fresh ingredients.

Eat more chocolate with Weight Watchers – working with Heinz to produce a new product range (left). A tasty and effective example of co-branding.

Ingredient brands

Ingredient brands take a key product component that conveys a specific benefit to the consumer to create a strong marketing proposition. Intel Inside is perhaps the most globally well-known ingredient brand as it supports Microsoft Windows. It enabled Intel to raise awareness among consumers of the microprocessor technology at the heart of their personal computer. Intel then gains brand visibility, which reinforces relationships with computer manufacturers and is associated with innovation. Another area is fabric ingredients, such as GORE-TEX® fabrics or Lycra, which are added to products to give better performance (whether that is waterproof and warmth, or spandex and stretchy). The 'ingredient' offers performance assurance for the customer and can affect purchasing decisions.

Alliances

Another form of collaboration is alliances, where companies connect under a new brand to provide incentives to customers through joint offers or by acquiring reward points. This is very typical of loyalty schemes and became popular when airlines joined in various networks to encourage customers to align themselves with their brands. These alliances then branched out to include other associations within the travel sector, such as tying in with car hire brands and hotels. The important thing to note here is that the group of companies under the alliance brand will associate itself with like-minded brands. So, for instance, an airline network may also choose to offer services from a five-star range of hotels to effectively promote a five-star experience.

GORE-TEX® fabric is a technical product that provides dryness and warmth in outdoor wear (top and left). It was first created in 1978 and has since been extended for outdoor leisure use, as well as workwear for emergency services through to military use.

The fabric is used by many brands, such as those which produce skiwear clothing, as an 'ingredient' with any purchase accompanied by the promise: 'Guaranteed to Keep You Dry® – if it doesn't, GORE-TEX® fabric will remedy the problem'.

Collaborating for innovation

Innovation is fundamental to the growth of any large brand. The old business model within the large companies used to be to seek out the best research and development (R&D) minds, hire them and retain them. If competitors looked threatening, the large companies would often buy them or out-do the smaller companies through sheer marketing muscle. Now, things are changing and 'open innovation' is becoming a new theme. This is an open form of collaboration where companies pay to seek expertise on product and service development with individuals and small providers, through online communities called 'ideagoras'.

Consumer goods company, P&G, now develops more than 50% of its innovations through outside collaboration. Its 'Connect + Develop' website, <www.pgconnectdevelop.com>, invites people to submit innovations to the company. Colgate-Palmolive paid US $25,000 to a scientist who suggested a new way of getting toothpaste into the tube. This kind of collaboration is dependent on experts, but it actively advances the idea of co-creation, where anyone is able to participate in creating new products.

To do

Partnership innovation

Partnerships can be used as a source of innovation for brands. But it can be hard to get the right ingredients. Think about which brand collaborations – co-branding ventures, alliances or affinity marketing partnerships – you like.

Consider the following:

→ What do you like about the partnership?

→ How does it make things better for the consumer? For example, does it offer a new product or service?

→ How does it enhance the brands of the individual partners? Is one brand benefiting more than the other?

→ What criteria makes a good partnership?

→ Can you suggest a new product or service based on an innovative partnership?

The rise of the ideagora

An ideagora is an online marketplace that offers companies and individuals the ability to tap into a community of ideas. It provides a new kind of platform to access talent and solutions to technical or R&D problems. In effect, this uses the idea of 'crowd-sourcing' to attract the brightest brains to solve problems. *BusinessWeek* described it as an 'eBay for innovation' (source: *BusinessWeek*, 15 February 2007, 'Ideagora, a marketplace for minds').

Ideagoras reflect the growing need for companies – particularly large corporations – to seek innovations and ideas from the outside, where previously they would have employed top R&D people to solve problems within the company. It also reflects the demand for innovation and the speed of change – companies need to constantly push out new products and innovations ahead of competitors. Consumer goods company, P&G, has publicly stated its commitment to 'open innovation' – it intends to source around 50% of its R&D efforts outside of the company.

The ideagora marketplace indicates a change in the way that business is done and the way that people choose to work. Top talent does not necessarily want to be employed – or constrained – by one company. Neither does that talent necessarily reside near the company itself – it may be in the technical institutes of Bangalore or in the universities of China. Cash prizes are offered for those who bring the solutions, while the company retains the knowledge and intellectual property that could lead to a successful product. It's a smart way of working.

Examples of websites for ideagoras can be found at: <www.innocentive.com> and <www.yet2.com>

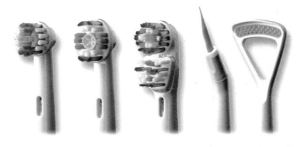

P&G's dedicated website, called 'Connect + Develop' encourages people to submit ideas or components for new products or services. Some of the many consumer products already produced by international brand P&G are shown here (above).

Affinity marketing

Affinity marketing seeks to develop a positive or influential relationship among customers by associations with other companies. These companies may be connected via a standalone brand. This association may offer better access to a group (or groups) of customers than by using conventional marketing techniques. These affinity groups can be commercial or not-for-profit.

The partnership goals

The objective may be to offer the customer a reward for being loyal, which helps improve customer retention rates, and can differentiate the particular brands within the market, as the consumer may prefer to buy the affinity brand. Another objective, as in the case of Product (RED), may be to reinforce charitable values as an element of the brand. The brand can also be enhanced through implied values within the partnership – for example, by connecting with a group of elite, high-end brands or with ethical brands.

Affinity benefits

Behind the scenes, an affinity partnership can also mean that resources are shared, so that operational costs (for example, of marketing) are lowered. The brands also benefit from joint marketing muscle – from their own brand, from the partner brands and through the affinity brand. Consumer benefits can include loyalty points that may open up other purchasing opportunities and discounts, or link to the personal values of the consumer.

Shared resources

The affinity brand's marketing as a group should reflect the consumer behaviour that the group requires. This could be:

Self-interest

The desire for personal benefit, such as serendipitous upgrades for travel or hotels, discounts on services, or added-value services.

Relational

A sense of belonging, where the consumer demonstrates an affiliation with the group, such as a specific hobby or breed of pet.

Aspirational

Links to desire to be part of a group because of its social implications. For example, many of the members of the Ferrari Club of Great Britain don't own a Ferrari but have a love for the brand and aspire to be a part of it.

Cause-related

A link to the consumer's personal values or empathy with a deserving cause or mission, such as Product (RED) and its goal to help women and children with HIV in Africa.

The affinity goal

Affinity groups can be defined by objectives and their motivation is to increase brand strength. They can be structured in different ways – for example, Saga is relevant to a particular demographic, by offering good rates for products such as insurance for the over-50s. Financial services are another common area for affinity partnership, particularly around payment cards. VISA, MasterCard and American Express all operate around affinity networks.

On the other hand, airline affinity networks such as Star, Skyteam and OneWorld bring together groups of airlines into collaborative marketing and code-sharing agreements, that also offer customer benefits through reward points (for free flights and other travel benefits, such as car hire). For charities, affinity marketing can offer a revenue stream. Charities tend to apply strict criteria to partnerships and associations with corporations, taking their membership base into account as well as their charitable status.

Affinity as loyalty schemes

Loyalty networks use affinity marketing to build broad and interchangeable benefits. The idea is that the link to an affinity programme will influence buyer behaviour when choosing a product or service. But these kinds of schemes have become less attractive among consumers where rewards may be difficult to redeem or require a volume of purchases before any benefit is felt. It is also debatable as to whether consumers will pay more for a brand to gain loyalty points or whether points are simply accumulated when the opportunity arises.

Case study
PRODUCT (RED)

(RED) is an example of a brand where each partner company – including Emporio Armani, Gap, American Express (UK only), Hallmark, Converse, Dell, Windows, Starbucks and Apple – licenses the (RED) brand and produces (PRODUCT) RED items. A percentage of profits from the sale of these items is donated to the Global Fund – which allocates the money to helping to eliminate HIV and AIDS in Africa, with an emphasis on the health of women and children. (RED) products include Apple's (PRODUCT) RED Special Edition iPod nano and shuffle, Gap's range of (PRODUCT) RED T-shirts, and the American Express 'RED' card in the UK.

In return, the company gains in reputation through cause-related associations, and also has access to a potential new consumer market – that of the 'conscious' consumer. (RED) is an innovative take on corporate charitable giving, where the brand partners with other companies to create (PRODUCT) RED branded items. To date, (RED) partners and events have generated over US $125 million for the Global Fund to help eliminate AIDS in Africa.

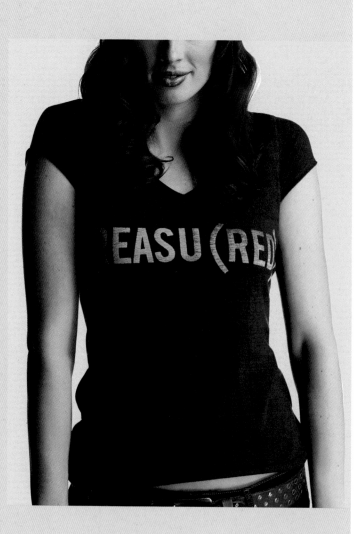

Part of the profit from RED branded products (above and left) is donated to HIV programmes for women and children in Africa.

Case study
Everyclick

Everyclick uses the web as a fundraising
platform for charities. Consumers can
use Everyclick as a search engine; to
shop online; create greeting cards; or
simply donate directly so that every time
the platform is used, money will go to the
nominated charity.

Everyclick offers an example of social
entrepreneurship where businesses are
created with a social goal as well as a focus
on business growth. It also offers a creative
way for companies or organisations to show
a commitment to social responsibility –
signing up to Everyclick means that they can
encourage employees or partners to donate
to charity.

Everyclick was set up in the UK and
currently teams up with 200,000 charities,
without charging the charities a fee. It
donates half of its revenue to charity.

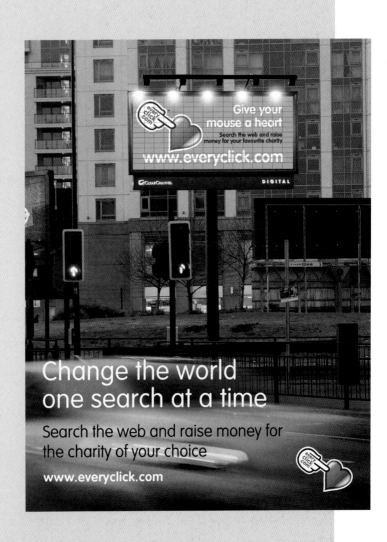

Everyclick offers a
technology platform where
charities can 'wrap' their
brand around a search
engine or donation page
to raise money (above).

The image (left) shows a
search engine page for the
development charity, VSO.

Charity-based partnerships

Partnerships between companies and charities or international organisations (such as the UN's WHO or World Food Programme) have become hugely popular with the growth of corporate social responsibility over the past decade. These kinds of associations come in all shapes and sizes: they may be long-term partnerships over five years that involve cash and knowledge transfer from the corporation; a community-based initiative; or at the product level, a cause-related marketing initiative where part of the product sale is donated to a charity.

In some cases, partnerships have emerged as an extension, or substitute, of sponsorship, where a company will choose to support a charity rather than, say, a sporting event. Generally, these partnerships will be created with sound business reasoning: they may be used to motivate and unite the employees of the company; to express brand values; or as a tactic to address an issue where the company may be vulnerable to NGO criticism – for example, the Coca-Cola partnership with the charity, the World Wildlife Fund (WWF). Any partnership should make sense to the audience and, ideally, successfully contribute to a need in society that can only be addressed through the joint knowledge and sharing of the partnership.

A fundraising tool

Still, for the charity sector, partnering as a concept is not new, as charities may use this as another form of fundraising. Some charities (such as Greenpeace and Amnesty International) refuse to partner with corporations; however, others such as WWF have a tier level of partnership with corporations, depending on the contribution made by the corporations.

Today, however, these partnerships are becoming more sophisticated, with corporations and charities seeking more long-term active engagement. This may involve tactics such as knowledge-sharing (often where the corporation provides knowledge) or technology transfers.

An example of collaborative branding between a corporation and charities is the HSBC Climate Partnership, a five-year partnership with NGOs that include the Climate Group, Earthwatch Institute, Smithsonian Tropical Research Institute and WWF.

The partnership sits distinctly within the HSBC brand, rather than working with other corporations. HSBC made an investment of US $100 million aimed at combating climate change by inspiring action by individuals, businesses and governments worldwide.

Case study
BA/UNICEF

Change for Good is a partnership between the airline BA and childrens charity, UNICEF. Since 1993, passengers on BA flights have been donating their loose change – from any currency – which is then committed to development projects for children around the world. It is now possible to donate online and in BA offices as well as in-flight.

The partnership is called a 'corporate fundraising partnership' which is a common term used today under the banner of 'corporate responsibility'. However, it was set up before many other companies adopted high-profile partnerships as part of their corporate responsibility initiatives.

In essence, Change for Good is a simple concept that probably originated as a public relations idea. As long-term initiatives, these kinds of partnerships can have a large impact for charities – to date, the partnership has raised US $25 million for UNICEF across 55 countries.

BA's partnership with UNICEF was set up in 1987. People donate their loose change, in any currency, while on BA flights. UK actor Michael Palin unveils a Change for Good plane to celebrate the partnership raising $25 million in 2008 (far right). Cabin crew play with street children at the Imbaba Girls Centre, Cairo (top).

BRITISH AIRWAYS
Change
for
Good
CHANGING CHILDREN'S LIVES
unicef ✿

Multi-stakeholder partnerships

These are partnerships where different parties – sometimes from business, NGOs and government – will link up to create a programme or initiative aimed at resolving issues in the sector. The multi-stakeholder element recognises that one company alone is unable to tackle the issue and, by working together, sector standards can improve and also provide a level playing field.

For example, oil and gas companies formed the Extractive Industries Transparency Initiative (EITI) in 2003 to tackle transparency and governance in the sector. Leading technology companies have formed the Global Network Initiative to address global standards on Freedom of Expression, prompted by media and NGO outrage over Yahoo! disclosing names of dissidents to the Chinese government. It is possible to identify at least one multi-stakeholder partnership (MSP) for any sector. What is new here is that it encourages conversation among companies that may not have happened a decade ago.

However, some NGOs are sceptical about the effectiveness of this dialogue, saying that it leads to more talk than action. This is valid criticism if the standards within the partnership are set too low, or if nothing is achieved. MSPs need to work to improve and change conditions in areas such as human rights and the environment.

North Star is a foundation that works as a collaborative brand, where partners tackle a core issue affecting their business operations together – the spread of HIV along transport corridors in Africa. Companies and organisations – including TNT, UNAIDS and WFP – collaborate under the North Star structure and brand to have immediate access to operational knowledge and resources for the transportation sector.

North Star's Wellness Centres operate across transport corridors in Africa. A roadside mobile health clinic in Malawi (top). A new clinic opens in 2009 in Mombasa, Kenya (above).

Farmers tending organic crops in Hubei Province, China, benefit from WWF's work on sustainable agriculture as part of the HSBC Climate Partnership (above).

A woman fishing in Lake Hong, China, illustrates sustainable practices promoted by WWF in its aim to protect 12,000 square kilometres of nature reserves (far left).

The Smithsonian Tropical Research Institute has reforested over 100 hectares in the Panama Canal Watershed since the launch of the partnership in 2007 (left).

HSBC Climate Partnership

Assessing the brand impact

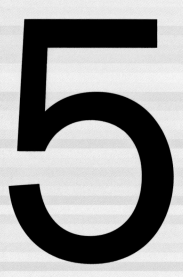

Why measure the brand?

Businesses like to quantify assets, to be able to ascertain what they are worth. But many business people still believe that a company's brand remains intangible and is unable to have a value attached. There are now a range of brand valuation tools, measuring everything from reputation to brand differentiation to online impact, that are created and used by branding agencies, advertising agencies, market research organisations and academics. Assigning a value to a corporate brand can improve the balance sheet if companies are being bought or sold and that brand, on its own, carries purchasing power. It can also boost pride in the brand among employees and encourage people to work for the company.

Measurement history

A strong period of mergers and acquisitions during the 1990s helped to expose the financial value of brands and gave impetus to the practice of brand measurement. One of the early valuations was around the drinks company, Diageo, which was created after a merger of Grand Metropolitan and Guinness in the late 1990s. Grand Metropolitan was a food and drinks brand that included Johnnie Walker whisky, Baileys, Smirnoff, Haagen-Dazs and Burger King within its portfolio. These are all brands with consumer loyalty that went beyond the value of the product itself and hence possessed a value that had to be quantified. However, even today, it is only acquired brands that show up on a company's balance sheet, rather than internally developed brands. This discrepancy fails to recognise the tangible value of some of the world's largest brands. Diageo has since sold off its food brands to position itself as a premier drinks business.

The dotcom era of the late 1990s represented an overvaluation of 'brand', where hype and a scramble to make fast money meant that many companies were being valued on ideas and name alone, without any substance. This led to the overpriced flotation of many a so-called dotcom company until, eventually, the bubble burst. However, a true brand valuation is much like financial analysis that factors in tangible aspects of the business as well as future risk — a brand based on hype alone would simply not cut it.

Measuring the brand performance

The increasing demand for brand valuation reflects the sophistication of the branding sector as well as the proliferation of different kinds of media. The ability to gauge how a brand is commonly perceived – both among customers as well as how it is conveyed and written about across media – is vital in judging how the brand or company is performing. Brand measurement and monitoring help marketing agencies (such as brand, public relations and advertising agencies) to determine whether the brand objectives are being met and, importantly, to prove their value to the client by showing what they have achieved.

What creates value?

While a company's share price can be an indicator of brand strength, it should not be viewed in isolation (and share prices are only applicable to publicly listed companies). A brand's success will be measured by the impact of the product, service and business that underpins the brand. This includes its perception and reputation among its stakeholders; the leadership of the business; its ability to differentiate and stay ahead of competitors; its ability to innovate and adapt; as well as its market share, margins, scale of presence and products sold. Measuring a brand's performance, therefore, is complex because a brand is affected by so much more than just financial indicators. Brand measurement is an in-depth topic in its own right and so you may find it worth reading about the subject in more detail if this is of specific interest.

Diageo is the owner of many world-leading drinks brands, such as the internationally recognised whisky, Johnnie Walker, and the liqueur, Baileys (right). Currently the top selling liqueur in the world, Baileys sold over 6.6 million cases a year by the end of 2003 – making it a leading export for Ireland, where the liqueur originates.

Apple's overall market share in the computer market has increased since the introduction of the iPod and iPhone (above) – products that have transformed the company.

In early 2009, it was reported that Apple has sold more than 17 million iPhones since June 2007 (*Register Hardware News*, 17 March 2009).

Market share as an indicator

A brand's market share is a figure that highlights the brand's purchasing power. It shows the proportion of people that buy into that brand, within its own sector. For example, in 2008, Nike had 36 per cent of the worldwide market share in sports footwear, compared to adidas's 21.8 per cent (this figure is based on Sporting Goods Intelligence, a directory that offers news, research and analysis of the sporting good industry). Strong brands will have a high market share but this share is also dependent upon the number of players in that sector and the type of sector that it represents. A market share can also fluctuate among leading brands, but it still offers an indicator of who is ahead.

However, a brand's market share alone can be misleading as a sole indicator of brand strength. For example, in the desktop operating system (OS) market, Microsoft controls around 80% of the market – a huge proportion in a market that has few players (Apple, and the open-source brands, Linux and Ubuntu are other players). However, Microsoft's dominant market share does not mean that its nearest competitor, Apple, has a weak brand. The reality is quite the opposite. Apple has had a loyal brand following since the birth of the company – importantly, however, it has significantly increased both its market share and brand perception over the past decade. To increase market share – and therefore, a customer base – is the goal of many companies.

All client relationships are built on respect and trust. The best relationships are the ones where you enjoy working with the client. But we, as an agency, still have to deliver and prove that we can add value to the business and inspire our client on a daily basis.

Adrian Burton
Creative director / Lambie-Nairn

Brand equity

As discussed, the value of a brand –
referred to as its equity – is determined
by a number of influences and factors. In
combination, these increase both the market
value of a brand as well as the measurable
value to the business. This is important
for any business as it determines what the
brand is worth if the brand is bought, sold
or licensed and also provides a business
case for investment in the brand – whether
seeking funding from external investment
or pitching for support from the
business itself.

Value in a name

Brand equity can be affected by a change
of details, be it a name change or significant
financial losses. The UK's Post Office
Group suffered badly when it renamed itself
Consignia in 2001, in a bid to compete in
an international logistics market against
companies such as TNT, DHL and Deutsche
Post. The press and public revolted and
16 months later, the name returned to the
rather dull (but nevertheless sensible) Post
Office Group. This reversion was probably
the right move; Consignia was a step too
far to substitute for a name that carried the
weight of its national heritage and operated
within a conservative market. The rebrand
also unfortunately coincided with a public
backlash against high-profile, expensive
branding campaigns.

In contrast, energy company BP took the
bold move of creating a new identity in
2000, replacing its well-known green shield
logo with a new brand mark, the helios,
supported by the message that BP meant
'Beyond Petroleum'. The change came after
British Petroleum merged with Amoco in
1998 and signified the company's shift from
operating solely as an oil company to its
transformation into an 'energy company';
indicative of the growing diversity of BP's
business to incorporate areas other than oil,
such as renewable energy.

The repositioning proved controversial. A
major oil company demonstrating concern
about reducing environmental damage
was deemed unconvincing by some, given
that BP's core business is oil exploration.
Since the rebrand, the company has
come under fire for its poor human rights,
environmental and health and safety record.
Its 'green' image lacks support among some
stakeholders, but the need to demonstrate
a more diverse energy business means that
the helios will probably stay.

BP is a well-known global brand, although it is still sometimes referred to as Amoco in the US. It continues to promote an environmental image and is also a key partner of the London 2012 Olympic and Paralympic Games.

A BP oil tanker refuels (top). A BP service station (far left). BP sponsors the Olympics with its 'Fuelling London 2012' campaign (left).

Brand as an intangible value?

A brand may seem to be a nebulous thing compared to the physical business assets, such as cash, products or property, that the business may own. However, less tangible attributes such as intellectual property, talent (that is, the people a company employs), and the company brand have now been recognised as both important and real assets to a business. What is more, a brand is as important for consumer-facing companies as for service brands, such as law firms or management consultancies, as it is often the brand that will differentiate the leaders.

From a consumer standpoint, some people will be prepared to pay more for a 'branded' product over another that may have exactly the same functionality or may even be an identical product beneath the brand; this has been proven to apply to products from cars to face creams. A popular brand can therefore carry a premium price tag and so substantially increase the overall valuation of its company.

Brand licensing and collaborations

Determining the value of a brand is also important in business deals where the brand is licensed. What is a brand worth when one company may licence the brand of another, particularly if the 'host' company is providing other benefits rather than the brand itself? Fashion and interior designers have long played on the equity of their own brands. It is a common tactic for top designers to lend their name, and specific designs, to department stores or retail brands. When international supermodel, Kate Moss, teamed up with the iconic fashion retail shop, Topshop, she effectively licensed her image, as her audience buys into her 'look' – her design skills are less important than her image. Moss signed a £3 million deal to design her own collection and, since its launch, her ranges have immediately sold out. Designer, or supermodel, collaborations may be expensive but can greatly boost the image of the host brand.

The Virgin Group forms many of its businesses through joint ventures and brand licensing arrangements; where other companies may provide the technological set-up and capabilities and Virgin 'lends' its brand to be licensed. Virgin itself carries the weight of a great name and message that people recognise; therefore, another company may gain significant market and audience access by working under the brand. Virgin Media formed in 2006 to offer Internet, landline, mobile and TV services as one package to the UK consumer; the result of a venture formed with ntl:Telewest, with Virgin licensing its brand to the existing TV service. At the same time, Virgin Media has opened up a new market for the Virgin Group. Virgin Mobile, a pay-as-you-go service in the US, is a joint venture with US telecoms company, Sprint, which operates under the Virgin Mobile brand.

Topshop was transformed
from a standard high-street
shop to an international
clothing mecca, initially
under the brand leadership
of Jane Shepperton. Its
profits have been boosted
since teaming up with
supermodel, Kate Moss, in
2008. Topshop opened its
first New York store in 2009.
Shown here are some of the
designs from the Spring/
Summer 2009 collection
(right).

Brand as monetary value

The monetary value of a brand – or its equity – is a total measure of the brand's impact on both the company and its market. This measurement is represented by its constituent elements in the diagram (right).

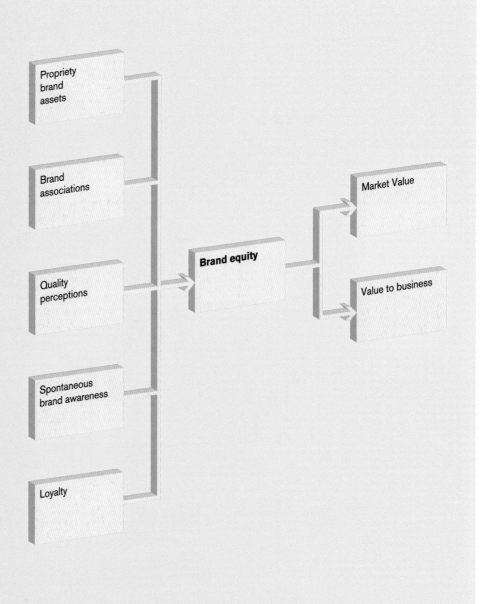

Shifting values

There are many ways in which brand equity can gain or lose value, often (but not always) impacting upon the company's share price. Negative impacts are usually associated with a loss of trust in the brand. This may be due to negative press, a high-profile court case (for example, if related to human rights abuses) or the loss of a key figurehead within the business, like the announcement in early 2009 that Steve Jobs would be taking a break from Apple's leadership. A drop in share price can also relate to unmet expectations – for example, if people were expecting a new product announcement from the company that never appears or is delayed.

Of course, some brands are routinely targeted by NGOs, website or guerrilla online campaigns for their unethical business practices or unsavoury associations. However, the degree of this impact on the overall brand status can vary. A strong brand can often withstand negative incidents or even turn them to its advantage. For example, the doyenne of US home living, Martha Stewart, encouraged her supporters to keep on buying from her stores while she was serving a prison term for insider trading. Her share price actually increased while she was in prison.

Surviving the press

A brand can also be held up as a 'poster child' if there is particular sensitivity around an issue – such as child labour. In 2008, the BBC's *Panorama* programme ran a story on low-end retailer, Primark, using child labour in its supply chain within the UK. This coverage led to further negative press, yet Primark continued to post record profits after the incident. A reason for the limited damage is that companies are now swift to act to address any negative press. Also, Primark is a low-end retailer and many of its customers prioritise price over issues about the origins of the clothes.

Alternatively, the public may have awareness that many mid- to high-end retailers similarly employ child labour to produce their clothing and thus feel that their options to find and buy ethically manufactured clothes are limited: Gap, for instance, admitted to child labour violations in thousands of outsource factories around the world in 2004; a story which resurfaced in 2007 with further reports of child labour in its production processes in India despite its rigorous social auditing systems launched after the first exposé.

However, it can still take years to rebuild trust in a brand where poor business practice has been exposed, as many banks have discovered in the wake of the financial crisis. Banks such as Swiss-owned bank UBS seemed to suffer more anecdotal reputational damage in its parent country because of its associations with Swiss national pride, than in the UK, where it had a strong financial presence.

Financial firm, UBS (above), suffered both reputational damage in its home country of Switzerland as well as financial damage during the 'credit crunch' crisis of 2008. UBS is the world's biggest money manager and reported heavy losses and 'write-downs'.

How to measure the
brand impact

The best way to measure the effectiveness
of a brand will differ among businesses.
A suitable measurement tool will depend
on the size and sector of the business,
its audience (e.g. whether it's consumer-
facing or business-facing), and relevant
measurement criteria. A small start-up
company is unlikely to apply heavily
sophisticated measurement tools that a
company such as Coca-Cola may use.

At the same time, there are other options
that can offer insight into a brand's
reputation and status without undertaking
a laborious task. Companies may choose
to look at the corporate brand, product
or service brands, and employee brand
as separate entities even though they are
obviously linked. Also, there may be different
impacts across the various channels (online
and offline).

Common insights

At whichever stage in the brand
development process they are, a company
could gain some useful insights into their
brand's performance by seeking answers
to the questions outlined on the
following page.

Brand influence

Why do people 'buy into' the brand? What do they perceive are its strengths? Are there any products that create the brand's identity? What status does the brand have among certain age groups?

Innovations

Do people consider any particular product or service as innovative? Can those innovations be used to extend the brand into other areas?

Brand communications

How is the brand being communicated? Which kind of communications do people remember? What have been the company's most effective campaigns? Do people remember the message or call to action? What do people think are the brand's values?

Sustainability

Does the brand have an underpinning sustainability strategy that looks at social and environmental impacts throughout the brand's life cycle? Should that strategy be communicated to the customer?

Differentiation

Can people recall the brand over competitors? How do people view the brand compared to its direct competitors? Does it stand out? Do people confuse the brand with the competition?

Online

Does the brand have a strong online presence? Does it have any online communities that may support it? Are there any negative online campaigns?

Leadership

Do any particular personalities behind the brand stand out? Is the brand based around a particular personality? If so, could that be potentially damaging for the brand?

Internal measures

What is the internal understanding of the brand values? What is the internal perception of the brand positioning and proposition compared to the competition? Are the brand guidelines being followed?

Easy ways to gauge the brand

To know what people think about the different elements of the brand (brand as a company, product, service or employer) is a useful process. However, a company must decide which feedback it will act upon, including how to build on the positive aspects, or make changes that will improve how the brand is publicly perceived.

Sometimes the best feedback on the brand will come from employees or other key stakeholders (such as customers or investors). Companies use communication agencies to keep up to date with what is being said about the brand. Some useful feedback can be found by employing the following resources:

Stakeholder dialogue

is a tactic used by communication agencies and consultancies to gauge a company's risks, issues and reputation among key opinion formers or other 'stakeholders' of the company, and may involve discussions with shareholders, employees, suppliers, investors, customers or the media as well as broader groups such as NGOs (charities) or industry bodies.

Employees

offer a great source of feedback about the brand. Any major rebrand should be undertaken with input – or, at a minimum – some feedback from employees. After all, employees act as the ambassadors of the brand. It will also be helpful to speak to suppliers and clients about their perception of the brand and service.

Online tools

can gauge a company's reputation or track online banter and so gain an understanding of people's perceptions of the brand; e.g. Technorati, Talkdigger, Google blog search or Yahoo Pipes. Some manual searching can determine whether the brand has a strong online presence, the support of online communities or any negative online campaigns.

A feedback facility

particularly on the company website is a useful tool to gather feedback and monitor factors such as service levels. People tend to use these kinds of facilities (that email directly to the company) for complaints rather than positive input. However, by doing so, any negative feedback is channelled down one route and can be acted upon.

Setting goals and KPIs

Measurement is only possible when realistic objectives and goals have been set. The desired objectives can be measured, but measurement need not necessarily be in quantifiable terms – it should also include qualitative links to the brand. Brand measurement could then relate to the following: market share and increased sales within a certain time period; reputation of the brand; deliverables on performance, such as product manufacturing; knowledge and awareness of the brand; and the accessibility of the brand, as well as its impact on competitors.

As brand measurement is not absolute, it is also worth tracking both tangible and intangible measurements over time to focus on the relative changes to the brand.

Knowing what people think about the different elements of the brand (brand as a company, product, service or employer) is a useful process. However, a company must decide which feedback it will act upon, including how to build on the positive aspects, or make changes that will improve a brand's perception.

Set objectives

The objective may set a goal five years on, but it should be broken down into annual objectives in order to reach the overall targets. A young, new brand may focus on raising awareness of the brand while an already well-established brand may aim to maintain a leadership position or increase its market position. An objective needs to be realistic and specific rather than generic.

Set realistic KPIs

KPI is a business term meaning Key Performance Indicator. Its purpose is to quantify a target by making it measurable. KPIs align with business goals and aim to assess performance. However, their use can sometimes be over-simplified, as it can be difficult to put a number against brand-related inputs, such as changes in perception or a rewarding brand experience.

Set timescales

Measurement needs to be done at regular intervals (without becoming an impediment to ongoing brand campaigns). Any objective should also have timescales attached. Phrase timescales in a language that is appropriate to the business and links back to the objective – for example, by aiming to increase the number of customers or clients by a certain year.

Brand measurement models

There are a number of different models for measuring brand value, from the esoteric to the analytical to the simplistic. Online measurement tools are also now popular as a way to gauge what people are saying about your brand by tracking the websites. This section highlights two of the key brand measurement methodologies – one from the global branding agency, Interbrand, which publishes an annual brand ranking survey with *BusinessWeek*, called 'Best Global Brands'; the other is a methodology created by advertising agency, Young & Rubicam.

Quantifying the value of a brand: Interbrand

Interbrand has a well-recognised brand valuation approach that has been established for a number of years. It attempts to apply quantitative and objective measures to rank the world's top brands. However, certain criteria must be met for the brand to be included: its internationality and turnover (Interbrand only considers large global brands), its audience and the data available – and so some well-known global brands (such as the BBC) will therefore inevitably be left out.

Interbrand looks at three key areas in their brand analysis:

Financial forecasting

The revenue that is generated from products and services. Interbrand analyses both the tangible and intangible assets of the business to determine their Economic Value Added (EVA). In Interbrand's 'Best Global Brands' report of 2008, EVA is described as a 'value-based management concept'. It determines the ability of the (branded) business to generate returns above what is invested into the business. To calculate this, Interbrand identifies the 'branded revenue' that is generated from products and services. It then deducts the brand's invested capital – such as its operating cost, employment bill and taxes – to get the economic value of the branded business.

How to measure the
brand impact

**Brand measurement
models**

Measurement in the
business and marketing
process

132–133

The role of branding

This identifies business earnings that are
attributable to the brand. This is dependent
on the sector in which the brand operates,
as the brand may be a key driver for
purchasing in the fashion or fragrance
sector, but may only be one attribute of
many in the business-to-business sector.
For example, while Intel has a strong brand,
many people will be using it because of its
bundling with Windows-based computers,
rather than necessarily choosing to
purchase an Intel-based computer.

Brand strength

This assesses the risk profile of the current
brand value. A risk profile may look at a
brand's future vulnerability in its particular
sector (for example, retail banking brands
are particularly vulnerable during the 'credit
crunch' period as people have lost trust in
these brands). This risk factor is discounted
from the brand's current value.

There are a number of factors that are
accounted for in the measurement process:
the brand's leadership, stability, market
dynamics, internationality, trends, support
and protection. In 2008, Interbrand's top
five brands were (in descending order)
Coca-Cola, IBM, Microsoft, GE and Nokia
respectively.

BMW consistently ranks
as one of the world's
leading brands – in 2009,
it was ranked as No. 13 in
Interbrand's 'Best Global
Brands' survey.

The car manufacturer is one
of the few car brands that
appeal to many different
kinds of drivers – from
the sports car enthusiast
to being a popular fleet
company car for its reliability.
It is now pushing the
low-emission message
and technology without
compromising the luxury
that is associated with its
range of cars (above).

Every year, international
branding agency, Interbrand,
publishes its brand survey,
which ranks the leading
brands in the world. Shown
here is the 'Best Retail
Brands' report for 2009 (left).

Young & Rubicam

International advertising agency, Young & Rubicam, have a well-known model called the Brand Asset Valuator (BAV) that is based on what consumers think about brands. It tracks the 'consumer equity value' of a brand, which is gauged from a comparative measure against its competition, based on an annual survey of 38,000 brands across the world. It is a valuation that also ties in with financial analysis so that the brand's contribution to a company's value can be determined.

BAV works in the following way: the 'Brand Strength' is based on 'differentiation' (D in the facing diagram or 'powergrid', signifying the extent to which a consumer will choose that brand) and 'market relevance' (R). This creates the brand's future value. In contrast, 'lagging indicators', which show the Brand's Stature, are based around the brand's 'esteem' (E) and 'knowledge' (K). Together, these four aspects of the brand demonstrate a pattern that can determine where the brand fits in the marketplace.

Brands at different stages of their life will tend to show similar patterns – for example, a young, recently launched brand will have low scores overall, while a new brand with strength will display strong levels of differentiation but not relevance. This methodology not only helps to gauge a brand against its competitors and better understand consumer perceptions, but also reveals whether the brand is in a healthy position to be extended.

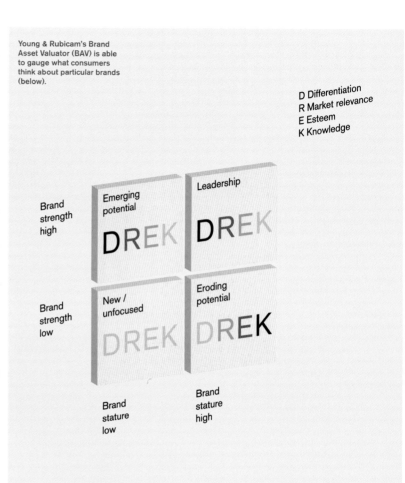

Young & Rubicam's Brand Asset Valuator (BAV) is able to gauge what consumers think about particular brands (below).

D Differentiation
R Market relevance
E Esteem
K Knowledge

How to measure the
brand impact

▼ **Brand measurement
models**

Measurement in the
business and marketing
process

135

Practising value-chain brand management is essential to establishing brand as a strategic business tool in the boardroom. This means using crunchy analytics of customer drivers to help shape brand strategies that are executed. These improvements are then tracked and integrated into the ongoing business management scorecard.

Iain Ellwood
Head of consulting / Interbrand

Measurement in the business and marketing process

Companies tend to look at the overall impact and value of a brand rather than assessing the direct impact of specific brand development activities. However, they can take actions that will add value to the overall brand of the business. There are points of maturity at each stage of a brand's development – from their start at birth through to later opportunities for brand extension. Each stage offers opportunities to measure brand equity, as well as increase brand recognition and loyalty.

Brand development

Increasing value in a brand is an evolutionary process rather than existing in a static relationship to its market. Therefore, brand strategies should be modified as knowledge and experience of the market and of a brand's customer base increases. The brand should also adapt to any significant changes in consumer behaviour and the purchasing environment (such as a recession). At each stage, market feedback, proactive research and measurement analysis may lead to a (healthy) review of brand strategy to ensure that the brand goes from strength to strength.

Birth of a brand

At the birth of a brand, the major focus is on clear positioning and establishing the name. Raising awareness of the brand includes actions such as advertising and endorsements, supported by other marketing activity (such as mail-outs, email campaigns or simple word of mouth) to encourage demand in the brand.

Second Stage

At the second stage, there should be clear and measurable market awareness of the brand as it becomes established. Actions to stimulate brand growth will focus on product or service evaluation as well as marketing. At this stage, attention must be paid to customer satisfaction to encourage customer loyalty and repeat purchases. Growth strategies for the brand will tend to focus on assessing quality, brand image, customer commitment and trust in the brand. Awareness of the brand will also need to be maintained.

Made its mark

A brand that has made its mark will begin to see that customer brand loyalty should be fairly resilient to actions by competitors. Spontaneous testing should show that consumer perceptions of quality and brand reputation align well with the original goals of the brand. At this stage, the brand should be in a position to support sub-branding or other brand extensions (if appropriate) so that brand equity can be built upon. The ultimate goal for many brands at this point will be to 'convert' people to their brand from competitors and so increase market share.

Brand measurement
models

Measurement in the
business and marketing
process

Understanding brand trends

136–137

To do	**Analysing the brand lifespan**

A brand will go through phases in both its perception and performance. It can be useful to map the lifespan of a brand to view how a brand has developed and responded to both external and internal factors as well as to tangible and intangible changes.

Choose a well-known brand (for example, Gap, Apple, Microsoft or The Body Shop), map its lifespan and provide recommendations for its future development.

Think about the following:

→ What is the brand currently best-known for?

→ What is its history and how has the brand performed financially throughout its lifespan?

→ How has the brand responded to difficult economic times – and also to good times? Did it launch new products and services or streamline its ranges?

→ Has the brand reinvented itself at any point? Why did it do so?

→ How has the brand performed compared to its closest competitor? Has it managed to out-perform at times? If so, why?

→ Has the brand fallen in popularity at all during its lifespan? If so, what seemed to be the reasons for this?

→ Did the brand face any negative media coverage? Was there an impact on share price?

→ Can you recommend action that the brand can take during difficult economic times or in another 'boom' market?

Brand futures

Understanding brand trends

The ability of brands to plan the future is critical to their survival. Brand managers need to constantly be aware of what is going on both inside and outside of their sector, and be open to changes in the wider technological, cultural, social and economic spheres. This foresight is important for both business and consumer brands, as every brand needs to adapt and innovate to remain relevant to their customer. But being in touch is one thing; applying knowledge and foresight to brand development requires skill, acumen and a degree of risk-taking.

Looking sideways

There is a tendency amongst many companies to track their closest competitors within a sector, to stay ahead of or match competitor products and service development. Another abiding tendency is to look at an iconic product such as the Apple iPod and try to emulate its success within the company's own products, by reflecting elements of its design or product capabilities. Staying up to date with developments is important, but the challenge is to apply original thought that is in line with the brand.

Great ideas can also arise from looking at the way that other sectors are innovating. For example, a footwear and apparel brand such as Nike or adidas may look at developments in industries as wide-ranging as pharmaceutical packaging to cosmetics brands to feed them insights and give them inspiration for their own products. Also useful is the trend of 'open innovation', in which companies collaborate with potential competitors, to combine know-how and innovation (such as a technology innovation) to produce something new. For example, the consumer goods brand P&G worked with a small technology provider to create the automated, electric toothbrush that spins at the touch of a button.

Measurement in the
business and marketing
process

▼ Understanding brand
trends

▷ The evolution of brands

140–141

Trends expertise

Some of the bigger, consumer-led brands will often use support from experts who work in the 'trends' sector, and specialise in analysing and predicting trends. This is a different area of expertise from traditional market research (although there may be some overlap in areas such as consumer insights) and is generally more qualitative than quantitative, because trends may talk in terms of societal insights rather than numbers.

Other companies, particularly the large consumer-led brands such as Philips Design, have a team working in-house that align trends with the direction of the business. This is essential for a global brand, where product and design development teams need to understand audience needs and trends across different countries to design and customise products accordingly.

A trends specialist should offer value to a company by identifying emerging trends across particular sectors, across different audiences (such as the youth market or over-50s) and across different countries. Today, the need to understand different cultures and markets is even more critical as brands emerge from nations such as China and as Western brands depend more on emerging markets. Product and service development must be adapted to local cultural norms as well as translate at an international level (the phrase 'global/local' is often used – meaning global management with a local twist).

Yet, identifying and predicting trends is just one aspect of the trends business. Insights must be interpreted and adapted to a brand in a way that is relevant to the business, the brand vision, to customers and within the market.

Nike is a company that leads with its brand and marketing. The company has integrated environmental concerns into its manufacturing process as a long-term goal.

The Pre-Cool Vest, part of Nike's urban sportswear range (above). A store in China, selling footwear that meets Nike's 'Considered' standards, created to minimise the company's environmental impact by 2011 (left).

Integrating trends into the brand development process

To adapt a significant trend to a business, a company needs to produce a convincing business case that aligns with the business and brand direction. It is often easier to introduce new ideas and methodologies within a smaller, younger company than it is in a large corporation. For a large company, a trend such as adapting to new online markets may require a significant shift within the business.

For example, if people are going to be buying newspapers less, then how can a media publisher shift its business to become digital? Media groups, such as the Guardian Media Group and News International have been steadily building up their digital presence in the past years, as readers move to the web for news coverage. *The Guardian* announced its presence on Twitter in March 2009. Now its 'followers' are able to receive up-to-date newsfeeds – it's an advanced move for a newspaper and one that will become commonplace. Newspaper and magazine titles are also on Facebook; their websites allow people to comment on articles or to email journalists directly, and many journalists blog in their own right.

Adapting brands to trends

Online markets have also matured as consumers now feel comfortable ordering goods and products over the web. Given this, should a high-street retail outlet switch its business to cater for online domination as its main source of income?

Electronics retailer, Dixons, closed its high-street shops to become a solely online business; Marks & Spencer sells a huge range of homewear online that is not available in-store; John Lewis, a UK department store, witnessed huge growth in its online sales throughout 2008, which made a healthy improvement to its profits. Other trends, such as social shifts to ethical consumerism and local shopping or technical, local-based services, may impact on the future of a company.

However, it is often difficult to make a convincing business case around 'what might be'. It takes confidence to introduce something new and different. Of course, some brands have bucked trends to lead the way. For example, the Apple iPod was introduced when many in the industry believed that MP3 technology was defunct. Neither is failure to move first into the market (the 'first mover') necessarily disastrous – as a new product or service may simply be better. Google's search engine came after AltaVista, Yahoo! and Lycos were already well-established, but has since dominated. Likewise, Microsoft's Internet Explorer (IE) pushed Netscape out of its previously dominant position (Microsoft's marketing muscle and IE's coupling with Windows helped).

Measurement in the
business and marketing
process

▼ Understanding brand
trends

▶ The evolution of brands

142–143

The unpredictable

Of course, not all trends can be predicted.
Unpredictable events may have the biggest
impacts on the collective or a national
psyche – such as the fall of the Twin Towers
in 2001 or the collapse of the global
financial markets in 2008. These kinds of
huge events can have an immediate impact
on how people think, act and consume.

After the events of 11 September 2001,
subsequent consumer research studies
showed that the dominant trait among
US consumers was fear – which affected
consumer buying habits. Following the
collapse of the US and European financial
systems, current consumer tastes have
shifted attitudes and behaviour away from a
consumer-driven spending society to one of
cautious – and conscious – consumption,
where conspicuous spending is suddenly
deemed both reckless and unfashionable.

Such dramatic and historical events
inevitably change the way that people
experience and respond to brands. They
may also cause sudden shifts in the brand
landscape as companies reform, collapse
or need rescuing. It seems incredible that
Citigroup, once the world's largest company
in the financial sector, has broken up into
separate businesses. Woolworths, the low-
end retail outlet, closed its 800 UK stores
in early 2009; the 300-year-old ceramics
brand, Wedgwood, faced liquidation.
Troubling financial times may prompt
closures, but these closures can also be
indicative of changing consumer tastes
and ways of spending; selling over the
Internet is becoming more appealing than
having a shop presence on the high street
for many brands, for example. Brands need
to constantly adapt to changing consumer
needs and new ways of purchasing.

Citigroup – which owns
Citibank (top and left) – was
the world's largest financial
institution until the financial
crisis at the end of 2008,
which led to the company
breaking up.

The presiding financial
downturn, which started at
the end of 2008, has been
compared to the crash of
1929 which led to the Great
Depression. The depth of the
financial crash has yet to be
played out – many emerging
markets and developing
economies are enduring
economic slowdown, which
is likely to increase global
poverty levels.

Case study
Philips Design – the future society / breaking down the trends

In 2007, Josephine Green, head of trends and strategy at Philips Design, wrote an insightful paper called 'Democratizing the future', which offers a vision of a future society based on current social and trend insights. She talks about business transforming itself to 'encompass social needs and social approaches', taking both social and cultural needs into account within business workings. This is a structure that was familiar during the Victorian era when companies played an active role in society, building schools, libraries and other community assets.

Green's reasoning is that Western society takes a linear view of living, that people are suffering from having too many 'things', and that we need to refocus our consumer/market-led approach to a people/social-led approach instead. According to Green, mass creativity, social innovation and sustainable development have become drivers of innovation. She projects an image of the 'context economy: where values are based on customisation, adaptability and transformation.'

By thinking in a different way, Green believes it is possible to '…drive a new era of creativity and growth' – a possible positioning for Philips as a company. The image may sound altruistic, but is in line with a move towards more sustainable business and the integration of corporate responsibility within business.

At the beginning of the 21st century, we have the possibility to enter a new social era – one in which the underlying ethos of sustainability and sustainable development helps to humanise and simplify our lives.

Josephine Green
Senior director of trends and strategy
Philips Design

The Philips 'green cuisine' kitchen concept (above) is an eco-efficient, hi-tech kitchen which revolves around a central table. Sensors mean that it is possible to cook or heat water anywhere on the table. There are also eco-efficiency features, like a composter that sits under the table, and water temperature controls.

Meanwhile, Philips' light blossom (left) is a brilliant concept in street lighting that acts as a source for renewable energy (generated from sun and wind) during the day and shines only the necessary light at night. It is aimed at reducing the reliance on energy by city-dwellers – who currently use 75% of the world's resources.

Measurement in the
business and marketing
process

▼ Understanding brand
trends

▷ The evolution of brands

144–145

...this is a great moment to
innovate: shrinking budgets
and diminishing revenues from
existing offerings normally bring
out the best and most creative
in business professionals.

Reinier Evers
trendwatching.com

The evolution of brands

While the fundamental principles of creating brands remain – understand and stay relevant to your audience – the world of branding is very different from that of 20 years ago. There has been an unprecedented pace of change in society, due to huge shifts in technology and global communications (after all, the Internet only reached mass audiences in the mid-1990s and the advent of email forever changed working life). This, in turn, has changed our relationship with brands. Not only do audiences have overwhelming choice today, but we can also choose the way in which we interact with brands – and whether to filter them, to engage with them through a variety of media, or to simply ignore them.

Audience evolution

This impact of global communications has increased our access to knowledge. Media exposure about company practices (or malpractice) and some high-profile company collapses – such as the Enron scandal of 2001 – means that people now openly question company behaviour as well as the products and services that they buy. We now have the ability to simply compare prices and shop for the best deal online, as well as to actually seek information about what lies behind products and services: including their ingredients, information about sourcing and a product's origins.

The media has also increased awareness around social issues such as obesity and the environment. A wave of celebrity chefs, such as the UK's Jamie Oliver, and TV healthy-living programmes, have prompted the public to ask questions about what they are eating and how they should eat. This, in turn, has influenced consumer consumption – the products offered on supermarket shelves look very different from how they did ten years ago.

This increasing audience awareness and knowledge does not essentially pose a threat to brands, but it does mean that brands need to maintain an authentic relationship between message and action, as well as endeavour to become more transparent than ever before. Over-exaggeration in areas such as 'green' product promotions tends to be exposed under the label of 'greenwash', which can ultimately impact upon a brand's reputation. Managing a brand is not only about making people aware of a product or service, but is also about managing a company's reputation.

Brands in a downturn

Economic downturns will inevitably influence consumer behaviour. Yet brands still need to innovate, advertise and communicate, even when times are tough – lower your profile and people will assume that your company is not doing well. History has shown that some of the world's most prominent brands started up in difficult times. During the Great Depression of the 1930s, brands such as Monopoly and HP emerged; companies such as Apple recovered after huge financial losses in the mid-1990s and many technology companies made it through the bursting of the dotcom bubble.

Economic ups and downs tend to be cyclical and can provide fertile ground for new brands to emerge – brands that adapt to new market conditions. The downturn that was triggered in 2008 by the collapse of financial institutions may be broad-reaching, but companies have had to readjust to difficult times over the past decade – the dotcom bubble bursting, the impact of 9/11, the collapse of the US housing market and, particularly, in the US, a 'culture of fear' that extends from uncertainty around the economy to fear of terrorism (according to Myra Stark at Saatchi & Saatchi advertising agency in 2004).

But the fact is that difficult times can lead to smarter moves in the way that business is conducted. New, national markets can also offer spaces for growth, particularly as the world's consumers are currently developing at different stages. Also, lean times offer an opportunity for smaller brands and service providers to do well, because they can offer quality and flexibility. A downturn can be transformative for both brands and audiences – things will inevitably improve but may do so with adjustments to behaviour and within a new consumer context.

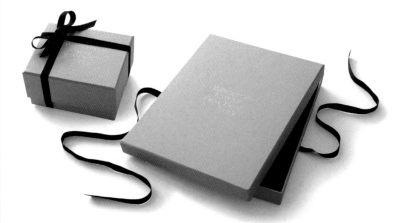

Rent Your Rocks is an online business that belongs to a traditional UK fine jewellery company, Winsor Bishop (above). It enables people to rent jewellery online for a special occasion at a weekly rental price. The concept responds to a shift among brands to introduce new business models that are sustainable, as people in the West now purchase less.

Creative evolution

The broadening sphere of branding and
its widening circle of influence now also
means that a brand is able to creatively
experiment more than ever before. How
people experience a brand can be affected
across many different touchpoints, and each
experience can add another dimension to
the brand. New areas, such as collaboration
through partnerships and innovation, offer
a broader territory for brands while sharing
the risk.

The ever-present need for brands to
communicate to a number of stakeholders
and audiences at any one time, across age
groups and countries, opens up a range of
creative challenges; from how companies
seek to reach existing and new audiences,
to how those audiences can experience
the brand.

Awareness of the different mindsets and
stages of audience development requires
a deep, insightful understanding into
prevailing cultural trends, different age
groups and diverse audience expectations.
From a creative standpoint, these are
exciting times, because there are so many
new ways and environments in which brands
can be interpreted today.

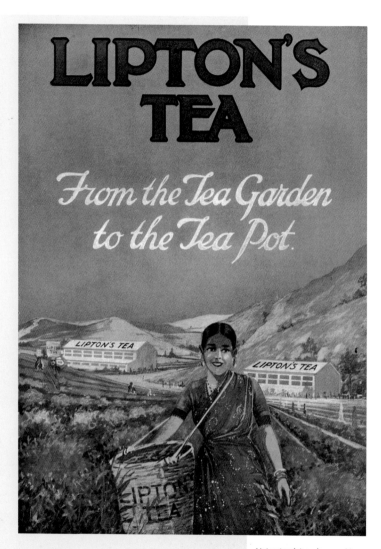

Lipton tea (above), owned by
Unilever, applies a process
through its brand that brings
corporate responsibility into
the core of its production
and 'route to market' by
reviewing the full life cycle
of the tea, from conditions
of the growers, through to
marketing and consumer
trends. They aim to have
Lipton Yellow Label tea bags
in Europe certified by the
Rainforest Alliance by 2010
and worldwide by 2015.

Case study
Unilever

Consumer goods company, Unilever, has introduced a methodology to integrate social, environmental and economic considerations into the brand innovation and development process. Called 'Brand Imprint', the methodology encourages the company to look at the business behind the brand: from the way it is produced, to working conditions, to changing consumer behaviour around brand consumption. The company seeks to source within developing countries. This makes ethical practice integral to the full brand proposition.

This is an incredibly innovative approach for a company as large as Unilever. Many companies now create environmental checklists during their R&D phase, but Unilever offers a holistic approach to brand management that effectively embodies a 'cradle to cradle' brand process that considers both environmental and social factors. The methodology has currently been applied to 15 brands. The message about the process is communicated to the customer only where the consumer is concerned about ethical production – for example, with Unilever's tea brands.

'For Lipton and PG Tips, our insight from consumers was that they directly relate the care in production and ethical sourcing to the function of the product. So there is an emotional benefit,' says the Brand Imprint creator, Head of sustainability Santiago Gowland. 'There is also a citizenship agenda for us – to bring the pickers and growers closer together with the drinker of the tea. We look at it as part of the complexity of building a brand. We also have strong values as a company, and doing the right thing is important to us.'

Unilever's founder, William Lever, started Lever Bros in the 1890s in Victorian England, to make 'cleanliness commonplace'. Today, Unilever owns some of the world's most well-known home and hygiene brands (above). Its brand mission is 'to add vitality to life'.

Key future trends

Brand culture has evolved at different times in different countries. It is dependent on a society's affluence, on the availability and public awareness of brands, as well as general accessibility to them (such as via the Internet). But branding is now a language that is internationally recognised and acknowledged, particularly as people travel more, countries open up to global politics and international trends (as amongst the former Eastern bloc countries, for example) and populations are exposed to new forms of media and communications.

The current global economic slow-down within markets like the US and Europe may lead to a more equal balance of power among countries, as nations such as China and India undergo substantive growth in their economy and middle classes. Spending in emerging markets is on the increase, while in Western markets it is decreasing. And although someone in Beijing will have a lower cost of living than someone in London or New York, these emerging markets offer opportunities simply because of their sheer size of population (there are 1.2 billion people in China to date and over 1 billion in India).

This section looks at some of the current trends that are affecting all major markets for brands.

Technology

There is no doubt that technology has changed our lives in the last two decades and will continue to have a large impact. Technology has now evolved to become much more integrated into our daily lives, particularly since the start of the millennium: for work communications, for personal lives, for shopping. While it makes life more convenient, it also speeds it up. Technology is also becoming a differentiator among generations (those who have grown up with computers versus those who have not), as well as within societal structures and countries.

Technology offers another dimension to the brand-building experience, other than the ability to sell more. It should be approached as a way to communicate and deepen the brand experience, rather than simply as a way to market. Brands will have to cater to changes in technology in the ways outlined on the following page.

Convenience

There is now an expectation among consumers that we should be able to receive information, products or services in any way we choose; whether searching for an address, information about a product, or to purchase online. This is a significant shift for brands when, previously, many people were concerned about online security and were reluctant to purchase products over the internet. Consumers now also expect that this convenience will be supported by an intuitive online experience, and that this experience will seamlessly integrate with the brand's 'real-world' presence and service. A negative experience, therefore, can damage the brand.

Location and knowledge-based services

The growth and sophistication of location-based services provides audiences with a new form of personalisation. This enables brands to target individuals based on where they are (by tracking their mobile phones). In practice, it's possible that brands may mainly use this technology to 'push' products or information to people. However, another use could be to better understand and profile audiences. At the same time we, as consumers, are able to filter out what we don't care to receive. We can switch off via technology, or mentally block out brands and choose to engage only with those that interest us.

A conversation

Brands need to offer customers the ability to communicate with them on a one-to-one level – audiences want to share views, to participate, and to be answered. The online channel offers a core means for a dialogue between company and stakeholder where companies are also given a 'right to reply'. Online formats give companies the opportunity to explore what is said about their brand. For example, the travel site, TripAdvisor, is based on people's own contributions and opinions on hotels, while <www.amazon.com> lets people review books and products and allows for comments from the author. Knowledge-based services such as news feeds, Twitter and other forms of short-hand communications also increase the dialogue between brand and customer, forcing a culture change within many corporations.

The online community

'Tribes', or communities, were being formed online years before the Facebook phenomenon, but sites such as Facebook, MySpace and Ning have taken this to a new level (in 2009, Facebook had more than 200 million active users). In the online world, communities connect people through their shared tastes, loyalties (such as Apple fans), politics or other means. These community models are appealing for brands – and government – as they can create supporters of specific communities: for example, by drumming up support around a particular product or by communicating shifts in business practice or policy. They can also be used by people to criticise brands and create momentum around a brand to change its behaviour (such as the anti-Walmart group on Facebook).

Amazon.com (top) started out as an online bookstore and now offers a range of product categories; consequently, it has turned a traditional sales business model on its head. Facebook (above) is the world's largest social networking site with over 200 million users worldwide (April 2009).

Community and collaboration

As traditional structures within society – such as familial and village structures – have broken down, new types of communities are forming. This is evident both in the real world as well as online. Local shopping, farmers' markets and cooperatives signify a return to more traditional ways of shopping and living. This way of living can complement more apparently convenient options such as supermarkets.

This move towards community-oriented companies and business practices represents a progression away from the individualistic, ambitious culture of the West during the last two decades, which many feel has led to social and personal isolation. This shift has also been encouraged, and often complemented, by online communities.

The return to a sense of community orientation also gives people a voice within a group, able to help instigate change; or work together on business ideas, while sharing any attendant risks. New ideas, novel ways of presenting products and services to people and creative ways of working will come about as a result of collaboration among companies and different kinds of organisations working across sectors, such as charities and government bodies joining forces together.

Sustainability

Increasing awareness about climate change and the impact of consumption on future generations has led to a 'tipping point' on 'green' issues. Companies are jumping on the green bandwagon as an area of innovation that may open their products up to new markets. Global leaders such as Barack Obama are pushing the 'green' economy and the creation of 'green-collar' workers as new ways to boost employment. Consumers, in turn, are becoming more aware of issues such as waste, water and recycling.

It is still early days, however, and there is still much debate over the right way to create a sustainable way of living. For example, biofuels were hailed as a 'green' solution, but have since been discredited due to the social impact of using land for fuel rather than for food. A company first needs to embed sustainable practices into its business before it can brand and communicate it.

Sustainability offers opportunities for business to cut costs, to become more efficient, to develop new products and services and offer simple, but innovative campaigns to encourage consumers to behave more responsibly. In turn, this will help businesses to improve their carbon footprint as well as their own business practices.

To do

Applying a trend to a brand

The ability to recognise trends is important to any brand manager. But it is more difficult to apply particular trends to the growth of a brand.

Select a key trend, such as the growth of social media or sustainability and choose a brand. Devise a strategy to apply that trend to the brand over the next three years and a relevant brand campaign.

Consider:

→ What do you think will be the growth of the trend itself? For example, is it likely to become a mainstream trend in other countries?

→ How do you think this trend will impact on the sector that your brand is in? Are there any indications to date of how the sector has adapted to the trend?

→ How do you think this trend will impact on your particular brand?

→ How do you think the company should respond over the next three years?

→ Come up with ideas, or a campaign, on how best to integrate this trend.

Consider the impact of the trend on the company brand, on the individual brands and at the product and service level. Also, think about the brand's different audiences and how the trend could be relevant to them.

A social conscience

Social issues such as health (obesity and disease), labour standards and poverty reduction can affect the commercial reputation of companies, and can have a knock-on impact for the brand. These kinds of issues can pose at once both a risk and an opportunity for business.

For example, any business with interests in South Africa has to consider the impact of HIV on its workforce and community (South Africa has the highest rate of HIV in the world); health issues such as obesity and health awareness are affecting brands in Western countries; and companies now actively engage with their supply chain to monitor production processes such as labour standards, to avoid incurring damage to their reputation.

At the same time, social issues offer opportunities for business. Brands can adopt 'cause-related marketing' campaigns, such as charity partnerships, to differentiate a product on the shelf. It is also easier to differentiate a company for its involvement in a social cause (such as disaster relief) than it is to stand out in the noisy 'green' space. There are also new market opportunities in the long run: companies (such as consumer goods brand, Unilever) actively involve themselves in development issues within their supply chains, as these markets represent the consumers of the future. There is currently a plethora of smaller 'ethical' brands emerging – that use sustainable materials in their products and that consider the environment and promote good business practice as a brand differentiator. There is no choice but for businesses to work towards integrating awareness and an accountability for the social and environmental impact of their practice as part of their daily business.

In 2008, celebrity UK photographer, Ian Rankin, worked with international charity, Oxfam, to raise awareness of the conflict in the Congo by taking images of refugees in Eastern Congo.

Internationalisation

Today's global picture has two key aspects
to it: it offers new and potentially huge
growth markets for brands; it also changes
the brand landscape as local brands move
into the international marketplace – brands
from 'new' markets such as China, Brazil
and India. This combination of factors means
that brand owners need to play in a much
more globalised way that is attuned to inter-
cultural differences and similarities.

Emerging markets are significant for
brands because of the sheer population
numbers that they represent. For example,
Interbrand's Aléjandro Pinedo says of Brazil
in Interbrand's 2008 'Best Global Brands'
report that: 'About 20% of the "D–class"
consumers were upgraded to "C–class,"
and this represents about 40 million people
in Brazil.' Many advertising and brand
agencies have long-established presences
in these markets, but it is only recently that
markets such as China have represented
significant opportunities for global brands
(spurred on by the Olympics hosting in
2008). International brands are often viewed
as elite brands in these markets, while local
brands still dominate among the masses.

Countering the invasion of international
brands is the rise of 'home-grown' brands.
As younger generations seek their own
identity, there is often an attitude to rely less
on 'foreign' brands and support or invest in
national brands; for instance, in countries
like New Zealand and South Africa, which
heavily promote locally made products
and encourage people to buy local. Brand
growth in emerging markets will not
necessarily imitate the Western-style growth
of the past decades, as culture plays a
significant role. For example, community and
status are still strong brand drivers in China,
compared to the West's predominant focus
on the individual.

Enamore is a fashion brand,
based in Wales, that has
sustainability at its core. It
uses organic, sustainable
and vintage materials to
create women's clothes and
accessories that are sexy
and fun, and produces the
clothes locally (above).

The fashion industry is
fast adapting to using
sustainable materials
in its production as well
as applying responsible
practices within its supply
chains, due to environmental
and social concerns.

Industry perspectives: digital

Ajaz Ahmed
Chairman and co-founder
AKQA

What has been the impact of digital technology on brands?

Digital technologies and profound shifts in consumer behaviour have levelled the playing field. Brands were created for producers. The web, by contrast, was created for consumers, to provide a way of picking through – and making individual sense of – masses of information. In the new environment, leading marketers have found alternative, arresting ways to make their brands connect with consumers. Brands that added value and inspire the consumer will be the ones that succeed.

Today, consumers are more inspired by immersive, unforgettable, interactive experiences that will not only capture that audience's interest and engagement, but will enhance the marketer's brand equity, sales and shareholder value in tangible, quantifiable ways. That is the ultimate lesson of the digital world. It's not what sounds good or looks cool that ultimately matters – it's what works.

What makes a great brand?

Modern marketing is not primarily about technology, it is about ideas and experiences that create talkability, provide real entertainment value or a useful service to the consumer, which is crafted with the same discipline as the product and as a result become indistinguishable. This is the future of marketing.

Brands that succeed in the future will pioneer these innovations and interactions. In approaching digital [branding], marketing executives have to start asking: what new capabilities and services will enhance the value of our brand to our customers?

To make this work, agencies have to bring together capabilities in content creation and distribution, interface design, e-commerce and new product development.

What do you believe is key to a good client/agency relationship?

Client companies will need to define more clearly the values that underlie the brand, and to instil them throughout – since every interaction with a customer will effectively become part of the brand. In that sense, the best agencies partner with their clients, delivering an idea, a product, a service, an experience, or an application, not a marketing mantra.

What is the current relationship between social media and branding – do you think that all brands should have a social media presence?

Social networks and other digital tools have become an indispensable operating system for people's lives and have enabled the easy, accessible creation of any individual's very own channel, sharing the information, content and updates they want with friends and family. The arrival of this 'channel me' – where people are interested in the automatic and relentless updates from their friends, family and the brands they choose to engage with – is having a profound impact on marketing; in addition to the fact that the more time people spend on social networks, the less time they are engaging with other types of non-interactive media.

Do you have any tips for branding students wishing to work in an agency?

We want to hire people who have an athlete's mentality, hunger and will. Steve Jobs made a speech where he advised students to 'stay hungry, stay foolish'. That's exactly what we look for at AKQA.

Modern marketing is not primarily about technology, it is about ideas and experiences that create talkability, provide real entertainment value or a useful service to the consumer ... This is the future of marketing.

Ajaz Ahmed
Co-founder / AKQA

Industry perspectives: brand strategy

Iain Ellwood
Head of consulting
Interbrand

What do you think will be the top three trends in branding over the next decade?

Firstly, regional brands will magnify or abandon their provenance in order to graduate to the global brand set. A new cohort of emerging (BRIC) market brands will graduate onto the world stage. They will collectively magnify or abandon their provenance in a bid to become a ubiquitous part of the global brand set. Brands like Haier, Tata, China Mobile and others will all have to navigate the decision on whether and how far to use their original provenance to build customer franchise beyond their shores. They will follow a tried and tested road of Sony, Samsung, Ford, BMW and others.

Secondly, brands will minimise downside risk through hybrid brand portfolio strategies. The default monolithic masterbrand strategies of the 1990s will be replaced with more selective hybrid strategies that minimise the risk of more dangerous product or market offerings. No longer will the Citigroup, Vodafone or AIG model of monolithic branding be the only solution. Firms will look to redefine their portfolio strategy based on risk as much as the usual brand attributes. This means that there will be more standalone brands creating detachment from the masterbrand to avoid unilateral damage if certain parts of the business suffer rapid brand degradation through failure or substantial losses.

Thirdly, a Return on Investment (ROI) based brand building. As brand strategy becomes a more strategic business tool, its methodology and tools will incorporate more value-based analytics. Return on marketing investment, customer acquisition and service costs will become the standard language of brand consultancy.

◀ Industry perspectives:
digital

▼ Industry perspectives:
brand strategy

▷ Industry perspectives:
innovation

158–159

Value-based brand management that integrates business performance metrics and establishes net brand-business contribution will be the Chief Marketing Officer's guiding principle.

What kind of brands do you think will be the leaders over the coming decade?

There is nothing surprising; those that offer genuine customer-driven propositions that are clearly differentiated from the competition and are delivered in a seductive experience. Brands like Apple, BMW and Nike will perennially lead the marketplace. For example, Coca-Cola has been the Best Global Brand in the Interbrand/ *BusinessWeek* league table for the past ten years.

The biggest difference in leading brands will be how rapidly they become leaders. Where previously brands may have taken decades or even centuries, new brands can become leaders in just a few years. Google, Starbucks and Ebay have all used strong customer advocacy and word of mouth to accelerate their rise to global brand leadership.

What would be your advice to students who want to work in branding?

Take a long hard look at yourself and ask: do I have these five talents?

1. Intellectual curiosity with mental agility
2. Obsession with customer behaviour
3. Empathy with business and finance
4. Superior language skills
5. Energy to drive things forward.

Finally, ask … What does my personal brand stand for?

The default monolithic masterbrand strategies of the 1990s will be replaced with more selective hybrid strategies that minimise the risk of more dangerous product or market offerings.

Iain Ellwood
Head of consulting / Interbrand

Industry perspectives: innovation

Matt Kingdon
Chairman and Co-founder
+ Kiran Wood
Brand Development Specialist
?What If! The Innovation Company

What does innovation mean for business?

MK: The idea of innovation within a company has changed from being only about product and service development to being seen as relevant to every business function and part of everyone's job – in marketing, sales and legal as well as in product and service development. Companies need to innovate – to do things faster, better and quicker. They also need to innovate to deliver brand equity across different models and distribution channels. Innovation is a broad concept that covers every sector.

What do you see as key influences in branding today?

KW: Consumers themselves are becoming more innovative and voting with their feet. An innovation culture exists in the lives of consumers – they have an expectation of new things. Individuals are also prepared to innovate themselves as the market entry is easier – anyone can set up a business online. So, the consumers of the future have the ability to just go out there and do it. Companies are also inviting people into their business. For example, Nike invited consumers to be part of the innovation team to test out snowboots, which was a new area of development for them. To do this, brands have to be less closed about their technology.

The principles of traditional branding are still important – brands need to stay true to themselves and be confident in who they are. There is a fast rate of change happening across the organisation so brands need to know what they are about. Brands have also moved from being intuitive to counter-intuitive – doing things that don't at first make sense. Google made its maps available for free so that people could link them to their websites – then Google charges a fee once there is a certain number of hits. Or Amazon selling second-hand books [when their core business is selling books]. Or companies like P&G now inviting their competitors in to be more collaborative. Innovation is moving higher up the agenda.

Is the current economic downturn changing consumer behaviour? What can brands do?

MK: People are becoming agile consumers. Those who once migrated upwards in terms of brand are now moving down to a lower price point. They are realising that the quality trade-off is not as extreme as they thought.

KW: The recession will influence people's value systems beyond this downturn. For example, we're seeing a rise in fast food and a decrease in healthy eating.

MK: A brand really has to do what it says it's going to do – it needs to deliver on its promise. Over the next few years, brand owners will be frightened off big thematic ad campaigns because consumers are too clever for that now. Brands will be stripped down to what we can compete on, rather than fluffed up with advertising. Instead, a brand needs to pick the standout feature and deliver on that, so that customers can be advocates of the brand. It's about really delivering on what will be important – prices can only be cut so far and there is less room on the shop shelves. Brands need to stick to good old-fashioned virtues and play that up. It's about not being afraid of who you are and shining a light on that.

KW: The brand experience is what will matter, rather than delivering a communications piece. Brands need to live up to their promises in a holistic way.

Brands need to stick to good old-fashioned virtues and play that up. It's about not being afraid of who you are and shining a light on that.

Matt Kingdon
Co-founder / ?What If!

Moving the brand forward

Our society is in the process of a transformation after enduring some rapid and shocking changes, such as the collapse of the financial system and the stark realisation that our resource needs will not be met if we continue to consume at our current rate. This is already having a huge impact on business.

It is likely that the coming decade will also be a transformative decade for brands as companies reposition during an economic downturn to offer products and services in new ways. New business models and areas such as the development of digital technologies will also inevitably affect the way that brands are being managed. A brand will need to stay relevant and true to its audience across a number of different markets and mediums.

The qualities of a good brand

Yet the key qualities of creating a good brand remain – the ability to formulate and deliver on the brand promise; to understand the ever-changing, knowledgeable customer base and market; and deliver a consistent and pleasing experience of the brand through all brand touchpoints.

Areas such as partnership and collaboration that potentially minimise risk will be on the increase, as will the need to measure, evaluate and recognise the return on brand-building investment. Measurement may be divided across the different channels of media and community. However, there is likely to be a resurgence in the need to gauge a brand's reputation and trust among its stakeholders, as this has become a key concern for consumers. Many people now look beyond the brand to understand the workings and reputation of the business behind it.

The emphasis in the coming years will also focus on how the brand is communicated. Brands need to continually communicate in an economic slowdown – rather than cut budget in this area. They need to communicate on issues such as environmental sustainability and inform consumers (and other stakeholders) how they are dealing with issues such as climate change. They need to communicate and adapt to new areas of technology to create new brand experiences and ensure that the brand is at the forefront of the next generation.

The impact of change

Many of the challenges faced by large brands today will also impact smaller brands as they grow and adapt to changing landscapes.

It is important that the fundamentals are understood at the outset of any brand building: clarity, consistency and simplicity in communications and execution are key, coupled with a long-term vision and the flexibility to adapt to an ever-changing brand environment.

The ability for a brand to remain authentic and true to its core values often becomes more challenging as the brand grows and expands. But today, in a world where communication is multi-channel and multi-dimensional, it is those brands that have a simple, strong message coupled with a great experience that will stand out. This also makes the brand easier to recall and for word to spread about it among those loyal to it. To achieve this, brands need to work with their audiences, to continually innovate and to remain true to themselves.

Rather than stirring up wants and creating false needs, successful brands will be those that provide the greatest positive contributions to those who are affected by their creation.

Kristina Dryza
Trend forecaster

Appendix

Conclusion

This book has examined the key principles that make up the fundamentals of branding. By exploring marketing concepts and trends, it aims to equip the reader with an understanding of how to apply these principles to the ongoing management of a brand.

The process of creating and developing brands is not necessarily a linear one. It requires good teamwork and an understanding of the many skills and disciplines that play a part in creating and maintaining a brand. For example, the designer needs to understand the writing and narrative process; the strategist must understand how the creative teams work; the creative team needs to understand the business vision and reasoning. Brand projects work well when each skill is translated to the other and there is a sharing of ideas and cross-working. Good teamwork also makes the process fun.

Essentially, however, branding is about communicating on many different levels. The brand must communicate to the audience in a relevant and effective way. There must also be clear communication from those who manage the brand, to its stakeholders. There must be good communication between the client and agency. And there must be effective communication within the brand creation team. A strong brand will also encourage its audience to communicate positively about it.

Any sustainable organisation needs ongoing brand management as part of its business. Branding is not a short-term, quick-hit process – a brand must be managed from its inception and throughout its lifetime. The launch is only the start. It is an area that is still evolving within many organisations, but is increasingly being understood as a fundamental part of any organisation. However, branding is not about following a trend or particular way of speaking. It is about innovation, translating ideas, understanding your audience, and communicating in the most effective way possible.

Take the time to build up your knowledge and experience of brands, no matter which area you choose to specialise in. Stay on top of the trends by staying informed of social and cultural influences, and of trends among the brands you see. Don't limit yourself to working with one client or one company – the best experience is gained by working across different brands and across different sectors. And seek inspiration for ideas from unusual places.

Branding is an exciting area to work in. Enjoy it.

A leap into the future with the brand, Howies (right) – a clothing brand now owned by Timberland. It carries the ethics and image of freedom, nature and sustainability.

◀ Moving the brand
forward

▼ Conclusion

▶ Student resources
Bibliography

166–**167**

Student resources

**www.adsoftheworld.com and
www.brandsoftheworld.com**
US-based sites run by www.graphics.com
and set up as a resource for creative design.

www.bannerblog.com.au
An Australian blog that was set up in 2005
to showcase online advertising, including
viral advertising that is worth watching.

www.brandblog.net
A blog dedicated to branding and marketing.

www.brandchannel.com
A weekly branding newsletter produced by
Interbrand.

www.brandrepublic.com
News and features on everything brand and
marketing.

www.cidoc.net
A site about corporate identity.

www.collings.co.za
The 'brand architect' blog written by brand
strategist and journalist, Patrick Collings.

www.coolhunting.com
For the insight into things that the
'coolhunters' like, crossing products, art,
culture, technology and design. The site
covers a range of categories including luxury
brands, hotels, clothing, fashion and the
handmade.

www.identityworks.com
Provides comments, reviews and insight on
corporate identities.

www.ilovetypography.com
For those interested in design and
typography.

www.innocentive.com
Example of an open innovation website.

www.interbrand.com
Interbrand's 'Best Global Brands' report.
Produced annually with *BusinessWeek*.

www.joshspear.com
New York and London-based, Josh is a
leading guru in youth trends, working with
some of the world's leading brands. His
blog discusses design, products and trends.

www.ministryoftype.co.uk
Good commentary on design and branding
from the UK, covering a range of topics and
examples of work.

www.palgrave-journals.com/bm
The Journal of Brand Management,
Palgrave Macmillan, leading academic
journal on brand management with articles
contributed by industry practitioners.

www.pgconnectdevelop.com
A website designed to invite consumers
to submit ideas or components for new
products or services.

www.saatchikevin.com
The 'inside' from Saatchi & Saatchi and
a link to the blog from the author of
'Lovemarks'.

www.superbrands.com
Creator of the annual 'Superbrands' and
'CoolBrands' lists.

www.trendwatching.com
A monthly trends briefing on consumer
trends produced in Amsterdam.

www.wgsn.com
An industry trends resource for the fashion
and style sectors.

Bibliography

David A. Aaker
Building Strong Brands
2002, Simon & Schuster Ltd; 2nd edition

David A. Aaker and Erich Joachimsthaler
Brand Leadership
2002, Free Press

Scott Berkun
The Myths of Innovation
2007, O'Reilly Media, Inc.; 1st edition

Michael Braungart and William McDonough
Cradle to Cradle: Remaking the Way We Make Things
2002, North Point Press; 1st edition

Leslie de Chernatony and
Malcolm McDonald
Creating Powerful Brands
2003, Butterworth-Heinemann

Melissa Davis
More Than a Name: an Introduction to Branding
2006, AVA Publishing

Iain Ellwood
The Essential Brand Book
2002, Kogan Page Ltd; 2nd revised edition

John Gerzema and Edward Lebar
The Brand Bubble: The Looming Crisis in Brand Value and How to Avoid it
2008, Jossey-Bass

Jeffrey Hollender & Stephen Fenichell
What Matters Most: Business, Social Responsibility and the End of the Era of Greed
2004, Random House

Robert Jones
The Big Idea
2000, HarperCollins Business

Philip Kotler and Nancy Lee
Social Marketing: Influencing Behaviors for Good
2007, Sage Publications; 3rd edition

Rick Levine, Christopher Locke,
Doc Searls and David Weinberger
The Cluetrain Manifesto
2000, Perseus Books, US; Reprint edition

Charlene Li and Josh Bernoff
Groundswell: Winning in a World Transformed by Social Technologies
2008, Harvard Business School Press

Adam Morgan
Eating the Big Fish: How Challenger Brands Can Compete Against Brand Leaders
2009, John Wiley & Sons; 2nd edition

David Ogilvy
Ogilvy on Advertising
2007, Prion Books Ltd

Wally Olins
On Brand
2004, Thames & Hudson

Wally Olins
Wally Olins: the Brand Handbook
2008, Thames & Hudson

Hamish Pringle and Majorie Thompson
Brand Spirit
2001, John Wiley & Sons

Don Tapscott and Anthony Williams
Wikinomics
2008, Atlantic Books

Glossary

Acquisition (see Mergers & Acquisitions)
When one company acquires the assets and rights of another. The brands may be integrated into the dominant company or the acquirer may choose to invest in expanding the acquired company independently.

Agencies
Companies that offer brand or other marketing expertise to service clients. These could be branding, digital, design or public relations agencies.

Audit
An 'audit' in the branding context often means an objective assessment of what branding assets collateral exists, the competitive position and the brand's perceived values.

Best practice
A piece of work that is recognised as representing the best way to apply the brand.

Brand
The public face, usually carefully constructed, of a marketable product, service, organisation or body. Brand is the interface between the organisation and the public.

Brand architecture
The topology of how an organisation structures and names the brands within its portfolio. This may involve product or service brands that sit under the corporate (company) brand, as well as sub-brands.

Brand associations
The feelings, beliefs and knowledge that consumers have about a brand based on their own experience of the brand.

Brand experience
A term used to refer to creating an experience when people come into contact with the brand. An experience may aim to reach all the senses.

Brand management
The discipline of managing a portfolio of brands, usually run by a marketing or brand manager. It was invented by P&G (Procter & Gamble) in the 1930s.

Brand manual
Acts as a guide for implementing the brand, often detailing areas such as logo, layouts, fonts and images.

Brand mark
The 'mark' or 'marque' that identifies the brand. It is also known as the logo and can include a strapline.

Brand perception
How a brand is perceived or viewed by its audience.

Brand values
The values that reflect the core of a brand. These are usually around five words that are used to embody and describe the brand to its employees. Values must be supported by behaviour.

BRIC
A term originally coined by Goldman Sachs to describe the four key emerging markets or new economies – Brazil, China, India and Russia.

Business-to-business
Brands that sell products or services to the business market rather than to a member of the public.

Channel (and media)
The medium or media format used in marketing the brand, e.g. television, radio, billboard, press.

Co-branding
When two or more brands appear together in marketing communications.

Communications
In the context of branding, the communications is the work which supports the brand campaign to inform people of developments to the brand, its values and messages.

Consumer
A buyer of the brand product or service.

Consumer-facing brands
Brands that sell products or services to the consumer market rather than the business market.

Consumer goods or FMCG
Fast Moving Consumer Goods relates to practical everyday products that people tend to use in the home. These may include washing, hygiene and beauty products. P&G and Unilever dominate this sector.

Cradle-to-cradle
Cradle-to-cradle describes systems – particularly in design – where the lifecycle of production has no harmful effects on the natural environment (rather than the 'cradle to grave' approach). It is used by many companies in their R&D and design.

Creative (development or execution)
An expression often used to refer to the 'creative' output of the brand including the design and words.

Demerger
When a brand is split from another to stand on its own. This often involves a name change and new identity for the new brand.

Equity
The value of a brand and its worth. Brand equity is based on the sum of all distinguishing qualities of a brand. It forms part of the company's balance sheet.

Freelance
A person who works as a contractor, either directly for a brand or for an agency.

Guardianship
The agency role of looking after the creative implementation of the brand.

Identity (the brand identity)
The way people identify a brand, which may include the brand mark (logo), its 'look and feel' and the experience with the brand.

Investment
People or a company that puts value into the brand for growth purposes.

Licensing
When a company has bought the right to market the brand, or an element of the brand, under its own name. A licensee will be the company that is 'borrowing' the brand; a licensor is the entity that owns the brand rights.

Look and feel
The visual style of a brand which encompasses the brand mark, colours, font and images. Together these create the overall 'look and feel' of the brand.

Marketplace
The brand's sector or market in which it exists. It can be the immediate competitor or the broader sector.

Mergers & Acquisitions (M&A)
The corporate finance term referring to the acquisition of a company (or a part of a company) or merging.

Narrative
A story that supports the brand.

NGOs
An acronym for Non-Governmental Organisation. These are charities that form part of civil society – that is, they are not part of the government.

Outsourced
When a company or agency uses outside help for a project. This may be done through a tender process.

Parent brand
The main brand owner or holding company.

Pitch
A presentation by an agency to a potential client to win a new account. This usually involves competing against other agencies and is, generally, a team effort.

Portfolio
The mix of brands within a company's brand architecture.

Positioning
Where a brand sits in relation to its competitors.

Product
A tangible, marketable item that is often the basis for the brand.

Proposition
The way a brand projects itself or what it says about itself.

Public sector
Government or government-related organisations that work to a different mandate from private companies or corporations.

Roll-out
The time it takes to launch the product, often from pre-launch through to post-launch phase.

Social media
Web-based and mobile ways to communicate, including online communities such as Facebook or MySpace.

Stakeholder
Everyone that the brand affects in the widest sense of the word; including investors, press, customers, employees and associations.

Strategy
The direction for the brand, which aligns with the goals of the business.

Sub-brand
A brand within a brand, for example, the iPod is a sub-brand of Apple.

Tone of voice
The 'vocabulary' and style for a brand, which also plays into the brand's style.

Touch-points
The points and interfaces where people come into contact with the brand.

Twitter
A social media network where people send online updates up to 140 characters long.

Visual identity
What a brand looks like including, among other things, its logo, typography and packaging.

Acknowledgements

There are many individuals and agencies who helped bring this book together and I am grateful to everyone who has contributed to the process – including sourcing images, interviews and editing.

This has included insight and images from individuals like the team at Lambie-Nairn, Robert Jones at Wolff Olins, Jeremy Hildreth at Saffron, Iain Ellwood at Interbrand, Ben and Emily at Bloom Design, Dan at Mystery, Ajaz Ahmed and Hester Bloch at AKQA and the team at ?What If! Thank you also to the charities and companies that provided images for the book.

A special thanks to Leonie Taylor for the laborious task of sourcing the images and to the team at AVA Publishing, including my editor Colette Meacher and Caroline Walmsley. Also, thank you to some great people who provided access to brands, quotes and insight including Sayula Kirby, Mark Mangla, Alistair Beattie and Kristina Dryza.

My deepest thanks go to Steve Everhard for his reading, input and sage words on every draft; to Hin-Yang Wong for his detailed and insightful feedback, and – finally – to my parents, John and Gill, for their unending support and to Franco for his patience.

Credits

Images courtesy of:

Gap p.13

Google p.14

McDonald's p.15

Philips © pp.16, 144

Cadbury's p.17

Huawei p.19

Haier p.19

NIKE, Inc. pp.21, 99, 141

Action for Children p.21

Mini p.22

Coca-Cola p.23

Audi p.27

Interbrand pp.32, 133

Saatchi & Saatchi p.33

Mr & Mrs Smith p.35

02 / Lambie-Nairn pp.37, 50

Virgin p.41

Tata pp.42, 43

The Body Shop p.45

Tesco pp.47, 62

Urban Outfitters p.49

Topshop pp.49, 125

Benetton p.51

The BBC p.53

Pret A Manger pp.54, 55

Harvey Nichols pp.57, 58

Aquascutum p.61

Marks & Spencer p.63

adidas. Source: Start Creative p.66

Royal Mail Group Ltd. 2008 © p.72

Toyota 2010 © p.75

Monocle p.77

Gaydar p.80

Stardoll p.81

American Apparel p.83

Howies pp.84, 85, 167

Greenpeace p.88

Hugues de Saint Salvy 'Green my Apple' artwork / Artifiction / <www.flickr.com/photos/justhugo> p.88

Peugeot p.89

<www.avaaz.org> p.90

<www.wikipedia.org> p.91

TNT World Food Programme © / Liz Maria Ubeda / Nicaragua School Feeding / April 2006 p.93

TNT Colour the World © / Roma Batryshin (Russia) / 2005 p.93

TNT Air operation of co-branded food parcels 2007 © p.93

Rizla Suzuki p.96

Omega p.101

Sainsbury's p.102

Use of the Heinz Trade Mark with the 'Weightwatchers from Heinz' logo is used with kind permission of H.J.Heinz Company Limited. p.102

Gore-Tex p.103

Procter and Gamble p.105

PRODUCT (RED) p.108

<www.everyclick.com> p.109

British Airways and UNICEF UK: Cabin crew play with street children at the Imbaba Girls Centre, Cairo, UNICEF / Egypt 2007 / Julie Milnes p.111

British Airways and UNICEF UK: Change for Good envelope focussing on water and sanitation, UNICEF / HQ06-1596 / Shehzad Noorani p.111

British Airways and UNICEF UK: Michael Palin unveils Change for Good branded plane to celebrate the partnership between UNICEF UK and British Airways reaching £25 million, UNICEF / Warren Potter p.111

World Food Programme / Edson Chagara © / roadside mobile health clinic in Malawi / 2006 p.112

TNT / Mubarak Adam © / PMAESA mobile health clinic in Mombasa, Kenya / 2009 p.112

HSBC Climate Partnership: Farmers tending organic crops in Hubei Province, China, © Brent Stirton / Getty Images / WWF-UK p.113

HSBC Climate Partnership: A woman fishing in Lake Hong, China, © Brent Stirton / Getty Images / WWF-UK p.113

HSBC Climate Partnership: The reforestation of the Panama Canal Watershed, © Christian Zeigler p.113

Apple p.119

Diageo Brands B.V. p.120

BP p.123

UBS p.127

BMW p.133

Citibank © p.143

Rent Your Rocks p.147

Unilever UK Limited. Lipton, Pears', Persil and Bovril are trade marks of Unilever PLC. pp.148, 149

<www.amazon.com> p.152

<www.facebook.com> p.152

Oxfam p.154

Enamore p.155

Lynne Elvins/Naomi Goulder

Working with ethics

The Fundamentals
of Branding

Ethical:
aware-
ness/
reflect-
ion/
debate

The subject of ethics is not new, yet its consideration within the applied visual arts is perhaps not as prevalent as it might be. Our aim here is to help a new generation of students, educators and practitioners find a methodology for structuring their thoughts and reflections in this vital area.

AVA Publishing hopes that these **Working with ethics** pages provide a platform for consideration and a flexible method for incorporating ethical concerns in the work of educators, students and professionals. Our approach consists of four parts:

The **introduction** is intended to be an accessible snapshot of the ethical landscape, both in terms of historical development and current dominant themes.

The **framework** positions ethical consideration into four areas and poses questions about the practical implications that might occur. Marking your response to each of these questions on the scale shown will allow your reactions to be further explored by comparison.

The **case study** sets out a real project and then poses some ethical questions for further consideration. This is a focus point for a debate rather than a critical analysis so there are no predetermined right or wrong answers.

A selection of **further reading** for you to consider areas of particular interest in more detail.

Ethics is a complex subject that interlaces the idea of responsibilities to society with a wide range of considerations relevant to the character and happiness of the individual. It concerns virtues of compassion, loyalty and strength, but also of confidence, imagination, humour and optimism. As introduced in ancient Greek philosophy, the fundamental ethical question is *what should I do*? How we might pursue a 'good' life not only raises moral concerns about the effects of our actions on others, but also personal concerns about our own integrity.

In modern times the most important and controversial questions in ethics have been the moral ones. With growing populations and improvements in mobility and communications, it is not surprising that considerations about how to structure our lives together on the planet should come to the forefront. For visual artists and communicators it should be no surprise that these considerations will enter into the creative process.

Some ethical considerations are already enshrined in government laws and regulations or in professional codes of conduct. For example, plagiarism and breaches of confidentiality can be punishable offences. Legislation in various nations makes it unlawful to exclude people with disabilities from accessing information or spaces. The trade of ivory as a material has been banned in many countries. In these cases, a clear line has been drawn under what is unacceptable. But most ethical matters remain open to debate, among experts and lay-people alike, and in the end we have to make our own choices on the basis of our own guiding principles or values. Is it more ethical to work for a charity than for a commercial company? Is it unethical to create something that others find ugly or offensive?

Specific questions such as these may lead to other questions that are more abstract. For example, is it only effects on humans (and what they care about) that are important, or might effects on the natural world require attention too? Is promoting ethical consequences justified even when it requires ethical sacrifices along the way? Must there be a single unifying theory of ethics (such as the Utilitarian thesis that the right course of action is always the one that leads to the greatest happiness of the greatest number), or might there always be many different ethical values that pull a person in various directions?

As we enter into ethical debate and engage with these dilemmas on a personal and professional level, we may change our views or change our view of others. The real test though is whether, as we reflect on these matters, we change the way we act as well as the way we think. Socrates, the 'father' of philosophy, proposed that people will naturally do 'good' if they know what is right. But this point might only lead us to yet another question: *how do we know what is right?*

You
What are your ethical beliefs?

Central to everything you do will be your attitude to people and issues around you. For some people their ethics are an active part of the decisions they make everyday as a consumer, a voter or a working professional. Others may think about ethics very little and yet this does not automatically make them unethical. Personal beliefs, lifestyle, politics, nationality, religion, gender, class or education can all influence your ethical viewpoint.

Using the scale, where would you place yourself? What do you take into account to make your decision? Compare results with your friends or colleagues.

Your client
What are your terms?

Working relationships are central to whether ethics can be embedded into a project and your conduct on a day-to-day basis is a demonstration of your professional ethics. The decision with the biggest impact is whom you choose to work with in the first place. Cigarette companies or arms traders are often-cited examples when talking about where a line might be drawn, but rarely are real situations so extreme. At what point might you turn down a project on ethical grounds and how much does the reality of having to earn a living effect your ability to choose?

Using the scale, where would you place a project? How does this compare to your personal ethical level?

01 02 03 04 05 06 07 08 09 10

01 02 03 04 05 06 07 08 09 10

Your specifications
What are the impacts of your materials?

In relatively recent times we are learning that many natural materials are in short supply. At the same time we are increasingly aware that some man-made materials can have harmful, long-term effects on people or the planet. How much do you know about the materials that you use? Do you know where they come from, how far they travel and under what conditions they are obtained? When your creation is no longer needed, will it be easy and safe to recycle? Will it disappear without a trace? Are these considerations the responsibility of you or are they out of your hands?

Using the scale, mark how ethical your material choices are.

Your creation
What is the purpose of your work?

Between you, your colleagues and an agreed brief, what will your creation achieve? What purpose will it have in society and will it make a positive contribution? Should your work result in more than commercial success or industry awards? Might your creation help save lives, educate, protect or inspire? Form and function are two established aspects of judging a creation, but there is little consensus on the obligations of visual artists and communicators toward society, or the role they might have in solving social or environmental problems. If you want recognition for being the creator, how responsible are you for what you create and where might that responsibility end?

Using the scale, mark how ethical the purpose of your work is.

01 02 03 04 05 06 07 08 09 10

01 02 03 04 05 06 07 08 09 10

One aspect of branding that raises an ethical dilemma is the trustworthiness of the brand messages. Are they an honest representation or an attempt to mislead and manipulate? If brand promises are broken or destroyed through scandal, hypocrisy or wrongdoing, trust is lost and a brand reputation can be ruined. Successful brands are built on truths; but do they, and should they, reflect the whole truth? A way that brands can become more ethical is by trusted brands using their relationships with consumers as a channel to raise public awareness. For example, a product brand may promote a charitable cause with an on-pack promotion. In some surveys, people have been found more likely to trust brands than governments, so there is potential to use that influence for good. But there is also certain scepticism that brands only exploit this route purely for commercial gain. Is it the responsibility of the branding agency to direct a client company toward a particular route or should this always be driven by existing company values?

Major corporations expanded dramatically at the end of the nineteenth century through mergers, consolidation and other forms of integration. The sheer size of these companies – the numbers of employees, the scale of their production, their resources and capacity for political influence – transformed society. The family, the church and the local community was suddenly dwarfed by these new giants, which required them to carve an acceptable place in people's minds.

One such company began in 1892, when Thomas Edison, inventor of the electric light bulb, merged various businesses to form the Edison General Electric Company. Charles Coffin, the first President of the company declared, 'The new merged company considers the public it serves first and the success of the company second'; and the first advertisement for 'the company' (rather than for one of its products) in 1916 was a declaration of its commitment to use electricity to improve people's lives.

Opening the doors by providing a 'factory tour' was one method that allowed the company to show itself at its best and could be used to promote a particular quality, such as the scientific sophistication of the production process. In 1919, Charles M. Ripley, who had previously written two classic works of welfare capitalism, travelled widely across America to deliver an illustrated lecture entitled 'The Romance of Power'. The tour, which continued for several years, invited people to witness the wonder of production that was the General Electric plant.

In 1922, Bruce Barton, considered by many to be one of the most influential advertising men of the 20th century, won the company's institutional advertising account. At the same time, a new management team believed that the future of the company would lie in the mass consumer market. To personalise the company, the word 'company' was dropped from the name and the GE logo was referred to as like 'the initials of a friend'. An 'electrical consciousness' campaign took shape in 1923 on the basis that GE shouldn't settle for just selling light bulbs, when it could instead claim credit for light itself. One series made a connection to women's emancipation by suggesting to women that their civic and political progress was intertwined with electrical progress. 'The suffrage and the switch' advertisement offered to 'help lift the drudgery from the shoulders of women' by encouraging the purchase of electrical appliances.

During World War II, the role of production for defence purposes meant that big businesses were held in high regard, perhaps higher than any branding, advertising or public relations campaigns could have ever dreamed of. General Electric, according to a survey in 1945, stood 'higher than ever with the public', with favourable views from 84 per cent of those interviewed. These businesses had already been part of society for two generations; the bewilderingly giant new corporations of the 1890s became simply ordinary, ubiquitous components of everyday life.

Today, GE is the only company listed in the Dow Jones Industrial Index that was also included in the original index in 1896. According to the Interbrand ranking of 'Best Global Brands' in 2008, GE held fourth position with the brand valued at over 51 billion dollars.

Does the creation of a brand encourage a false public perception of what a company is?

Is it ethical or unethical to connect a company's reputation with wider social issues, such as women's rights or the provision of light?

Would you work for GE?

I think in many ways the world is now over-full of brands, over-full of hype, and over-full of information. The word 'brand' sometimes fills me with horror. And the fact that I am possibly one myself is even more horrific.

Paul Smith

Further reading

AIGA
Design business and ethics
2007, AIGA

Eaton, Marcia Muelder
Aesthetics and the good life
1989, Associated University Press

Ellison, David
Ethics and aesthetics in European modernist literature
2001, Cambridge University Press

Fenner, David EW (Ed.)
Ethics and the arts: an anthology
1995, Garland Reference Library of Social Science

Gini, Al (Ed.)
Case studies in business ethics
2005, Prentice Hall

McDonough, William and Braungart, Michael
'Cradle to Cradle: Remaking the Way We Make Things'
2002

Papanek, Victor
'Design for the Real World: Making to Measure'
1971

United Nations
Global Compact the Ten Principles www.unglobalcompact.org/
AboutTheGC/TheTenPrinciples/index.html